KEYS
TO THE CAGE

ABOUT THE AUTHOR

Sue Leonard has been a full-time freelance journalist for eleven years. She writes for the *Irish Independent*, the *Irish Examiner*, the *Evening Herald*, *Reality* and *Face Up* magazines, and *Books Ireland*. Originally from Hampshire, she trained for two years as a nurse at the Middlesex Hospital in London. As a health journalist she has twice been congratulated by Headline, the National Media Monitoring Programme, on her sensitive, accurate and responsible reporting. She now lives in County Wicklow.

KEYS
TO THE CAGE

HOW

PEOPLE COPE

WITH DEPRESSION

Sue Leonard

NEW
ISLAND

KEYS TO THE CAGE
First published 2010
by New Island
2 Brookside
Dundrum Road
Dublin 14

www.newisland.ie

ISBN 978-1-84840-065-8

British Library Cataloguing Data. A CIP catalogue record for this book is
available from the British Library.

Book design by Sin É Design

The title *Keys to the Cage* has been adapted with permission from an extract
from *Prozac Nation* by Elizabeth Wurtzel, Quartet Books (1996)

Printed in Ireland by ColourBooks

New Island received financial assistance from
The Arts Council (An Comhairle Ealaíon), Dublin, Ireland

10 9 8 7 6 5 4 3 2 1

For Michael, for everything

CONTENTS

ACKNOWLEDGEMENTS

Warmest thanks to all at New Island, especially Edwin Higel, Deirdre O'Neill and Inka Hagen for your belief and expertise. To my wonderful agent, Jonathan Williams, for nurturing the idea and for spotting jargon. To Gráinne Killeen, a true tour de force. To Irene Feighan, Vickie Maye, Siobhan Cronin and Jack Power at the *Irish Examiner*; Frank Coughlan, Rowena Walsh and Helen Hanley at the *Irish Independent*; Dave Diebold at the *Evening Herald*; Fr Gerry Moloney at *Reality*; and Jeremy Addis at *Books Ireland* for all the work over the years. Not forgetting Katie Donovan, who started it all. To Gerry Hickey, Paul O'Brien and Cleo Murphy for the contacts. To my children, Josephine, Tim, Lucinda and Rebecca, for your patience; and to Thomas, Max, Louise, Daisy and Alex for providing diversion. To my mother, Joy Almond, and my sister, Penny Lakin, for lifelong encouragement. To my friends, especially Denyse Woods, Susan Calder, Pippa Coughlan and Marian Kenny for your unending support. But most of all, to the fourteen people without whom this book would simply not exist. Thank you for your honesty, your courage, your warmth, your humour and your good company. Thank you for sharing your stories.

PREFACE

Depression. Panic. Anxiety. Despair. Stress. Black dog. Call it what you will, depressive illness in Ireland is escalating. It is estimated that one in four people will suffer from depression at some stage in their lives. Yet it is still largely misunderstood. As a doctor's daughter, a former nurse and a medical journalist, I have encountered many people in difficulty and despair. I have seen their helplessness and heard their anger. People with depression are all too aware that misunderstanding leads to stigma.

When the genesis for this book came in March 2009, all the talk was of downturn, of recession, redundancy and repossession. This, we were told, was causing a pandemic of depression. Facing bankruptcy, businessmen lost all sense of self. In despair, some considered suicide. People rang radio stations and described crippling panic attacks as they faced life with a diminished income. No wonder experts believe that by 2020 depression will be the second most burdensome illness on health services in Ireland, the first being heart disease.

When someone has depression, they retreat into a dark world. Unable to express their bleakest thoughts, they feel terribly alone. They cannot sleep. They worry incessantly. Every problem becomes a crisis, their thoughts spiralling in a loop of despair. Their view of life is skewed; they believe their life has no meaning. They are stuck in an altered world and nobody understands, not even the people who love them.

And that is the problem. If you are close to a sufferer, you feel scared too. You feel you're living with a shadow of the person you knew. There is a different look in their eyes; a change in their speech pattern. Their senses seem dulled. It can be terrifying.

The sufferer may have panic attacks. They may feel unable to drive, unable to work, or even to function from day to day. They might spend all day in bed. Being close to the sufferer, you worry. You are scared to leave them, even for a few hours. You are scared of what they might do.

You are desperate to help, but you don't know how. You feel trapped, frustrated, even angry. You want to scream, 'Pull yourself together.' You know that is neither wise nor fair, that it's the worst thing you can do, but sometimes the words pop out anyway.

You start to share their fears, to believe in the bleak scenarios they paint. It is hard to tell what is truth, what is fiction. And if you're not careful, you will be pulled down too into the spiral of panic. It is like spinning, tangled up together, out of control in a washing machine. You start to believe that life, as you knew it, is over.

You talk to friends. They're full of support; they listen and console. But you need to talk to someone who knows: someone who has been depressed or has been affected by such illness. But there's that stigma. People are scared to talk. There is a reluctance to acknowledge the condition.

You almost wish the illness was physical. At least then the treatment would be clear. The broken leg could be set, the cancer treated with chemo. Mental illness is more complex. Should the sufferer have antidepressants? Should they have counselling? And if so, what kind should they have? Do alternative therapies help? Does meditation? Should they go on a special diet? Everyone you ask has a different view.

As I write this, the climate could be changing. Early in 2010, Marian Keyes wrote about her current, crippling depression. She said she was living in hell. Her brave words have sparked discussion. Perhaps understanding might follow. Certainly, the people featured in this book hope so.

All fourteen have suffered from distress or panic, sometimes for years on end. They were all keen to talk. Some of them felt frustrated that their illness has been hidden from the public gaze, frustrated too at the treatment they had received. They have told their stories with great courage, with humour and humanity. Parts of their stories are distressing. But they are ultimately full of hope. Their experiences show that there is an end in sight. There is help and there are solutions.

The stories are diverse. Pauline is seventy-one and bereaved, Keith is just twenty. Ryan suffered abuse at home, Senan at school. Ned and Geraldine's panic evolved from redundancy and job stress, Emma's evolved from exams. Margaret's panic began when she was pregnant, Valerie hit rock bottom after the birth of twins. Luke had problems 'coming out'. Orla, who is naturally vivacious, struggles with the stress around her multiple sclerosis. They have different stories, different solutions, but there are commonalities too. And the main one, running through every account, is that people just don't understand. And that, some of the sufferers contend, includes the 'experts'.

Keys to the Cage was written for everyone affected by depressive illness. It's for those who suffer. Reading these stories, they will feel less alone. At the end of each chapter the lists of 'The things that helped' and 'The things that didn't help' will give sufferers strategies for managing their recovery.

The book is also for those close to a sufferer. For partners, children, parents, friends and colleagues. It is for everyone who wants to understand depression; for everyone who wants to hear it from the 'real experts' – the sufferers themselves. My hope is that it will shatter the stigma.

Sue Leonard, County Wicklow, January 2010

CHAPTER ONE
Emma

Emma* is twenty-nine. A scientist who works at Trinity College Dublin, she embraces life. Yet six years ago, Emma had a mental breakdown. She had been suffering from depression for nine months at the time and, in despair, she attempted suicide.

*name has been changed

The year 2002 started well for Emma. A fourth-year student at Trinity College Dublin, she adored her course in science and was expected to do well in her exams.

'I'd had a great four years,' she says. 'I'd lived at home throughout that time. I wasn't a party animal; I wasn't out every night of the week, but I had an active enough social life. I did well there, but I didn't overachieve. At school I'd always been in the top five. I won academic awards every year, but I quickly realised at Trinity that I wasn't that special. And I was okay with that. I just wanted to be better than average. Just before the exams, though, my mum was ill in hospital. We weren't getting on well at the time. We have a close relationship; we share a birthday. We get on famously, but when we row it's ferocious.

'I would be studying all day long, then I'd go in and see her. She'd give out to me for only being there at two in the afternoon. She'd say, "Why weren't you here at eleven o'clock?" It got very messy. I felt dismissed, as if my stress wasn't valid. One day she was giving out and we had a huge row. I had the overwhelming feeling that, as a daughter, I was not good enough. I was not loving Mum the way she needed to be loved. I felt that even if I got super grades, my parents would not be happy. I was doing something wrong somewhere else. No matter what I did, it would be wrong in the eyes of one or both of my parents. And that was a horrible feeling. I went home and fell apart. I remember lying on the kitchen floor all afternoon just howling. It was a short sharp breakdown. It was incredibly acute, but it blew over very fast.'

Emma had been a happy child who excelled in sport and had good friends. 'I was a perfectionist, and I was quite sensitive. There was a lot going on in my childhood. My father was an alcoholic from before I was born until I was fourteen. He was never violent, never an angry drunk, but alcoholics can be incredibly manipulative. My parents broke up when I was eleven. I didn't appreciate at the time that that was having an effect on me. But I did get used to sacrificing myself to my father. He came first. I thought, if I behave better, he will love me more. And I thought that, maybe, he would stop drinking. I'd confront him sometimes. I'd refuse to get into the car, but I was never a rebel. My teachers thought I was fantastic, but I was probably growing up way too fast.

'I called my dad after my mini breakdown because I felt I needed the support of a parent. I needed someone to tell me that I wasn't going crazy. After what Dad had been through with his multiple attempts at getting dry, I felt that he would understand. And he was great. He hadn't anything magical to say to me, but he didn't judge me. He didn't really have any reaction, but that was good. He just said, "Okay. This is happening." And he rang a family friend, a psychiatrist. She then rang me, but by then I felt embarrassed. I suspect she thought there was a "drama queen" element to it. And I felt awkward talking to her because she was my mum's friend, and therefore her sympathies lay with her. I felt guilty.'

Knowing she would not get a second chance at those exams, Emma picked herself up, carried on revising and did well in her finals. She then set off for Hawaii with her boyfriend, to spend what promised to be an idyllic summer working in a science lab. 'We were living the dream. I loved the work. There was a pool in the back garden, and we spent all our spare time scuba-diving. But I was waking up every other morning crying. I was homesick, but I couldn't understand what was going on in my mind. Why was I so upset? I just didn't get it.

'When I returned home to Ireland at the end of the summer, I told my mother how bad I'd been feeling. And my mother suggested that I see my doctor. Luckily, I trusted my GP absolutely. I was incredibly lucky. She'd done further studies in mental health issues, dealing with depression and related illnesses. I went in, sat down and just talked to her.

'Straight away she said, "Emma, you're depressed." She was so accepting about the whole thing and told me that she had had depression too. She said that she knew how it felt and that it was okay to feel that way. It was an illness and it was treatable. That was amazing for me to hear. I had huge admiration for her. She is successful and perfectly normal and functioning. I thought, if she can get through it, then so can I. I remember feeling so relieved. I had a name for it. I was not going crazy but had something that other people had.'

> ❛ I was so lucky that my GP understood. I have spoken to so many people since, and their doctors have been incredibly dismissive. There is a fear, amongst people, about going to a GP. So many people report bad experiences ❜

Emma's euphoria was short-lived. That evening, while chatting to friends after she had been scuba-diving, one mentioned that some of his relations were depressed. 'He said, "I wish they would just shut up and get on with it." That was when it hit home. I realised this illness is something which carries huge stigma.

'I was prescribed with the antidepressant Effexor XR 75. It took a while to work, but after two or three weeks when the drug kicked in, I did begin to feel better. Meanwhile, I had weekly sessions of Cognitive Behavioural Therapy.' (This is a form of psychotherapy that helps people to find new ways of thinking and behaving to deal with their problems like depression and anxiety.)'I had six sessions, but at €70 a week it was expensive. My family helped out with the cost, but I didn't feel I could continue with it indefinitely.

'In October 2002, I started a PhD in Dublin City University. That meant I had to live some distance from family and friends. I was in a new environment. Everything was brand new. I felt completely out of my comfort zone. I struggled on but found life pretty difficult. And at Easter 2003, my grandmother died. I was devastated. Her loss had a huge effect on me. It was the first death I had known. A cousin and myself were my granny's favourites. She was especially proud of me. I could always rely on her to say something nice.

'Life at this time was very complicated. I wasn't enjoying my PhD programme. I was struggling with it. The Effexor didn't seem to be working any more. I went back to my doctor and she gave me a higher dose, but it didn't really help. I was still feeling bad. One day I started crying in the lab. That was really embarrassing. People didn't know how to cope. How could they?

'At that stage I'd officially broken up with my boyfriend from college days, the one who'd come to Hawaii, but we were still seeing each other. It was a destructive relationship. He was a nice guy, but he didn't know how to stand up to me. I have to watch myself. I can be manipulative. I can revert to childish behaviour, and I need strong people around me; people who can tell me to cop on and to stop behaving badly. We were having a relationship, but not actually calling it one. One night he stayed with me, but two days later he came over to say he had met somebody else and wanted to be with her and not me. That was the ultimate rejection. I found myself in my apartment thinking, I cannot take this any more. It was overwhelming. I really couldn't imagine being able to face the future or to get through it. I went and found all my medication and took the lot. I didn't really know what I was doing.

'I didn't feel there was anyone I could call. At that point I felt people were getting sick and tired of me. Here I was, nine months after I had been diagnosed with depression and I still wasn't better.

People who have not had depression have a limited tolerance of it. They think, "how long can this go on?" Logically, it makes no sense at all. I did think about ringing the Samaritans, but I knew they wouldn't give me a solution. I was beyond talking. I just needed a way out.

> ❝ It still irks me when people say that suicide is selfish. Because when you are in that situation, in your head it is the most unselfish thing you can do. You genuinely believe that if you remove yourself, you are doing everyone a favour. You think you are the biggest drain on everybody ❞

'After I'd swallowed the pills, though, I became extremely scared. I felt stupid. I thought, how much of an idiot can I be? I tried ringing my ex-boyfriend. I knew his sister was staying with him, and she's a doctor.

'Luckily she was there. And she took me to the Accident and Emergency Department at the Mater Hospital in Dublin. They called my father too. He came in, but my mother was away on holiday at the time. Dad didn't judge me. He sat with me, wanting to make sure I was okay. When Mum heard, she wasn't as understanding. She did tell me a couple of times that I had done it to get attention.

'And there was an element of that, though not in a flashy "look at me" way. I suppose I was trying to tell people that I still wasn't well. At that stage, talking to them didn't seem to be getting the message across. I didn't need my stomach pumped out. I hadn't taken enough pills for that.' She laughs. 'I couldn't even do that right! They kept me there for four hours under observation, then sent me on my way. Nobody came down to talk to me. They just told me to go to my GP. I went home by myself, feeling such a failure. All I had done was cause huge upset to all the people I cared about. And now they were more than likely angry with me.

'I went to my GP the next day, and she was amazingly supportive. She said, "We need to take a different approach." She changed my medication to Lexapro 10. She sat with me for ages. She said, "The darkest hour of the night comes just before dawn." And she also told me, "I think this is your turning point." She had such belief in me. At that point, she was the only person who did. That was the beginning of the road back to recovery.'

Emma was advised to examine her life and to make positive changes. She decided then to discontinue her PhD. 'That was heart-wrenching. I felt such a failure. I've always been an achiever, and though my parents weren't really pushy, they were proud of me when I did well. I talked to them, and they said, "We don't care what you do as long as it makes you happy." Having their support in this made all the difference to me. It stopped me from feeling so guilty.'

Leaving science, Emma changed tack and started working as a retail manager at a store in Dublin city centre. 'It was a frivolous job. It was easy, and I couldn't fail at it. That was such a relief. I moved back to south Dublin, close to my family and close to the sea; I'd missed living on the coast. Being close to the sea is important to me. Most importantly, perhaps, I finally walked away from my former boyfriend. That summer I met someone new. I felt so much better by then, and in the autumn I cut the dose of Lexapro by half. And by February 2004 I came off it altogether.

'Two weeks later, my new boyfriend dumped me. The day after it happened, I walked around the Botanic Gardens and something told me I would be okay. It took a while, but I got through it. I told myself, if I can survive a break-up without medication, I can cope with anything.

'Two thousand and four was a bumper year for me. I went off to South America for the summer. I was teaching scuba-diving just to please myself. And when I came back, I began a Research

Masters in Science in Trinity. I got back into sport. I went to the gym and I started to eat well and to look after myself. The medication had caused me to lose weight and then gain it. I have never been skinny. So working in retail alongside all the stick insects had been difficult. There had still been an emphasis on "the skinnier I can be and the prettier I can be, the more successful I will be." I am over that now. My life since then has gone really well. I have had another bad break-up, but I coped fine. I know now that it is not all my fault. But I recognise that I choose people who are a bit broken. I try to fix people. I have to be careful about that. I am very happy being by myself at the moment.

'I now work in Trinity. It's a great place to be. I could never leave! It's an administrative job, and I love it. I'm big into sport too. I lift weights. I'm good at it and now lift competitively. And it's something that I do entirely for myself, to make myself happy.

> ❛ I manage to stop slipping back to really dark places by accepting that I will get things wrong sometimes ❜

'I'm aware that I'm still susceptible to stress. If I had a massive upset, I am prone to getting bad again. I'm a little sensitive. I still wonder if I am good enough to do certain things. I still don't put myself in a situation where I can fail greatly. I avoid something I know I will not cope with. There have been times that I have been in danger of slipping back into bad thoughts. Being aware that that could happen is really important for me. I check in with myself, just saying, "this is happening," and I need to look at what it is in my life that is causing it. Then I make a conscious decision to do something about it.'

The stigma of depression, Emma says, makes life much worse for a sufferer. 'I was very careful whom I told. Doing the PhD, I constantly felt that my work was just not good enough. And because the people there knew that I suffered from depression, I was too embarrassed to ask for help. I would love depression to be more acceptable to people. I would love the awareness to be better. I'd like to stamp out the continued misconceptions. Even the term "mental health issues" has connotations. That makes it tough to find help. There is little information available about psychiatrists and psychotherapists. Their qualifications can vary widely, and it can be hard to find out who is good and who is not. You can ask around for a good dermatologist, but if you ask about a psychiatrist, people do a double-take and wonder what is wrong.'

> ❝ The very worst thing you can say to someone who has depression is, "you will be grand." That invalidates what the person is feeling. It compounds everything ❞

If someone tells you they have depression, how should you react? 'Talk to them. Ask them about it. And don't dismiss it. When people come out with news like that, their friends tend to shy away and feel embarrassed. When I spoke about it and people actively asked about it, I felt, this is great. I can talk about it. That was so comforting.

'And when someone says, "I know someone who suffers" or even, "I have suffered myself," that is just amazing. You know they have some kind of understanding about it.'

The things that helped

My GP
■ Having her to talk to made all the difference to me.

Drug therapy
■ That got me back to a place where I could start coping. But there were side-effects. With Effexor XR, I felt sick every day from two p.m. onwards. I couldn't eat.

Lexapro suited me better. I think that's because there were anti-anxiety pro- perties, and anxiety is something that I'm prone to. I barely knew I was on it, but on both drugs my sex drive was right down.

> ❝ I like to be good to myself for no other reason than because I want to be. I'll walk down to the Farmers' Market in Dun Laoghaire on a Sunday morning for a California Market Bakery muffin ❞

Cognitive Behavioural Therapy

- This was good, but six sessions were not really enough. I would have had more if I had been able to afford it. I had begun to explore why the depression was happening, but I did not really have a chance to put my coping mechanisms in place. It did help, in that it was somewhere to go and bawl my eyes out without being judged.

Internet forums and discussion sites

- At my lowest point I took a huge amount of comfort from an online forum. It was anonymous. It gave me a sense of calm to read other people's stories. It stopped the isolation. But as soon as you realise you are better, it feels like an indulgence. You realise, I am wallowing now. That is the time to stop.

Support from friends

- I never attended a support group, but a couple of close friends were a great help to me. They still are. There is one I turn to if things are difficult and I need perspective.

The things that didn't help

Counselling

■ I went to a counsellor and she asked me about my dreams. I thought, please stop it! The scientific side of me did not like it. I walked out thinking, I feel no better. For me, the problem with counsellors is that I find it difficult to talk to someone unless they help me to find some kind of solution. That is why I liked the Cognitive Behavioural Therapy. It gave me coping skills.

Emma's Advice

1. Don't be afraid to talk. Never be afraid to ask for help.

2. Go to your GP. If he or she is not sympathetic, go to another one.

3. Realise that other people have been through the same thing. Read about famous people with depression such as Winston Churchill, Leonard Cohen and Emma Thompson. Find out how they coped.

4. Trust someone when they say you will get better.

5. Don't be frightened to take antidepressants. They should get you back to a place where you can start coping.

FOR MORE INFORMATION:

Cognitive Behavioural Therapy – www.icbt.ie.

Antidepressants –
www.irishhealth.com/clin/depression/antidepressants.html

CHAPTER TWO
Anthony

Anthony from County Sligo suffered from severe depression. This began when he was in his late teens. It became so bad that he was unable to function. He felt suicidal for a while and made several attempts to take his own life. Now aged thirty, Anthony is doing well. He is still on medication, but he has learned to manage his condition.

When Anthony was 19, he jumped from the second-floor window of a disused hospital. He was a patient in St Columba's Psychiatric Hospital, Sligo, at the time, and had entered the old hospital, an abandoned building, on the same site.

'The building had been derelict for years,' he says. 'When I went in there, I had decided to end my life. I didn't know what I was going to do or how I was going to do it, but I wanted to end the pain. Killing yourself is not a selfish thing to do; you don't want to hurt your family. It's not brave either. It is neither of those things. My thinking just wasn't right.'

❝ No doctor, and no pill, can guarantee that you will never suffer again. If you are dead, you are not suffering any more ❞

That wasn't the first time Anthony had tried to kill himself. He had been feeling suicidal on and off for the past two years. Now, though, he thinks of that last attempt as his turning point.

Anthony was a happy child. 'But I was always quiet. I had five sisters. I was the second youngest in the family, and I got on particularly well with two of my sisters. They were much more outgoing than me. I got on well with my Mum too, but when arguments came along, it was always me and Dad against my sisters and Mum. There were fights between my sisters as well, but I didn't like conflict of any kind. Our council house was small. I didn't have my own room. The girls shared a room, but I had to sleep on a couch in the sitting room. That bothered me, especially later on. I had nowhere to keep my stuff and could never put up posters. I had no room to bring my friends back to and no privacy. That was tough. But it wasn't like there was a choice.

'I was pretty happy at school. I was a bit of a joker, but I was intelligent enough. I wasn't a genius or anything, but I was good enough at all my subjects. I was always active and fit. I played football and hung around with a few boys, but I didn't have a large circle of friends. When teachers asked me what were my good points, I always said, "I'm a great listener." My family would have described me like that. I wasn't too proud of it back then, but now I see it as a positive thing.

'When I was thirteen, I remember going to the Gaeltacht in Spiddal. It was the first time I'd spent more than a few days away from home. I was only there for three weeks, but as a teenager, Jesus, that was a long time. I was shy. I was reserved and that bugged me. I didn't enjoy it down there, but I didn't tell anyone. I was bullied a bit at that time by older guys, but no worse than anyone else. It was subtle bullying. I couldn't do anything about it. Kids in your own area can think they are better than other kids. They'd say things about my family or the size of my house. I never felt I was singled out, but of course it bothered me. It didn't exactly make me feel good.

'I did fine in my Leaving Certificate. I remember I got an A1 for Honours Irish. I went to the Sligo Institute of Technology in 1996 to study mechanical engineering. I was very dedicated to the course and at the end of the year I got an A grade. At college I hung around with three or four guys, but I didn't have a girlfriend. I hadn't had one while I was growing up. I thought, "What would I say to a girl?" I used to go to nightclubs from when I was sixteen. But when I was heading back home on the bus, I wouldn't feel well at all. I wanted to get away from people. I was dying to get home so that I could hide under the covers.

'In the summer after first year, I worked for a builder. It was someone I knew. I'd been at school with his son. And that was when I became really anxious. I felt paranoid. I thought that people were laughing at me. I was very sensitive to that. If you imagine something like that, it might as well be real. My concentration was going too. It was hard to focus on my work. My stomach would feel empty, as if I was really hungry. The back of my head would heat up. I'd feel this pressure. I always knew that it wasn't physical; that I wasn't going to die. I thought, this is all in my head. I know now that I was suffering from panic attacks, but back then I didn't know what the attacks were. I didn't think there was anything that could be done about it. I didn't tell anyone. I thought this was the way I was going to be for ever.

'When I wasn't working, I'd be lying in bed staring at the ceiling. I'd do that for hours. My parents noticed. So did my sisters. They were worried. They said, "Go to a doctor," but I said "No." I didn't think that anyone could help me. I'm not sure why I felt so bad. I was probably telling myself I was stupid for twelve hours a day. I remember I didn't want anyone to take any photos of me. I was frightened they would then see how bad I was feeling. I didn't want to go back to college; I didn't want to be around people, but I went in that first day. I imagined that everyone knew about me, that they were all laughing about me among themselves.

> ❝ To say that I felt lonely doesn't describe it. You can be surrounded by people, but you are alone ❞

'I left college at lunchtime. I remember I walked around the town for two or three hours. I went down to the docks. I didn't know where I was going or what I should do. I didn't feel good. Eventually I got the courage to ring my sister and explain to her what had happened. She drove into town to collect me. I didn't go back to college. My family didn't know how to deal with me. I wouldn't open up to them, so they had no idea what was going on. They knew I was down, but they didn't know how bad it was. My friends might have realised something was wrong, but I'd never been the life and soul of the party. My decline was gradual. But sure, they must have noticed.

'I remember my Uncle Michael calling down to the house. I didn't know it back then but he would have done voluntary work with the Samaritans. He took me down to the doctor. My own GP wasn't there. It was another doctor but she was grand. She asked me a few questions. She asked how was my mood. I wasn't in a great place. My uncle would have said a few things for me. My head was down. I wouldn't make eye contact with people. She suggested that I go into hospital. She sent me to St Columba's Hospital in Sligo. I'd heard of it, but I didn't know anything about it.

> **❝ I was thinking about death all the time. It was, "If I could stop the pain, I won't have to suffer any more. My family won't suffer. I'll stop bringing them down." ❞**

'I might as well have been sent to prison. From being a prisoner in my mind, I was now a physical prisoner. I probably could have left any time I wanted, but I knew even if I did leave, I wouldn't have felt any better outside. They kept an eye on me. I remember there was a window the width of the door, like a spy-hole. As they passed by, they would look in. I was in a single room like a cell. It was horrible!

'At the start they brought my food to me. Then I started eating in the canteen. I got on okay with a few of the patients. There was one guy the same age as me. He was German. I remember him. But a good few of them were older; they were fifty or sixty. I didn't feel any comfort in there at all. I was thinking that the doctors and nurses were laughing at me. They put me on medication, and at the start I had side-effects. I'd have a dry mouth and feel a bit dizzy. I was there for six weeks, but it might as well have been six years. I couldn't see myself ever improving enough to get out.

'I didn't have the words in my head to say how I was feeling. There were forms to fill out to say how you were from one to ten. One said "how is your sex drive?" I hadn't any interest in sex just then. How do you pick a number to say how interested you are in life? There were no minus numbers. I was ticking number four because I didn't want to seem like a freak. I wouldn't tell them anything. I wouldn't know how to.

'I did get out eventually. I went back home to my parents' house. I was on Amitriptyline and Zyprexa. I was on Inderal as well. For the first few weeks I had a dry mouth and a buzz in my head, but after a while my body got used to the drugs. When I got out, I didn't feel too bad, maybe the same as when I finished my first year in college. But I wasn't great. My body was all tensed up. I went back working for another friend who was a builder. I didn't feel great but I kept at it. But I had no hopes or ambition for the future.

'After five months I was admitted to hospital again. This time I'd taken some tablets. I'm not sure how many I took. I don't think I was planning suicide. My thinking wasn't right, but I thought if I took more tablets than I'd been prescribed, I would get better quicker. I wasn't alone at home when I took them. I told everyone I'd taken seven or eight, but actually I had taken a lot more. This time my dad drove me in. I remember I couldn't focus on the nurse's eyes. My head was slumped down to one side. After two or three days the doctor gave me an injection. I don't know what was in it, but within two hours a lightness came to my body. It felt strange because I hadn't felt good in fucking ages. It seemed to come from nowhere. I thought I'd be that way for ever. I was only in hospital for a week. I was happy. I was getting to know the other patients.

'I was on the same medication as before when I came out. For five weeks I was on top of the world. I was working full-time in a kitchen, and I was happy to be there. I was going out a lot too.

Then I went on holiday to England with my favourite sister, a friend of hers and her friend's boyfriend. It was amazing that she was letting me go with her. I'd hated myself until that point, and now people were accepting me. That was good enough for me. I didn't know, but I was elated. I was probably good to be around, even though I was hyper. It was "Come on, look at me!" It was an unnatural high, but it felt good.

'We were only in England for the weekend. While we were there, I smoked hash – just joints with other people. But from the elation, I came crashing down. On the boat coming home, I wasn't interacting with anyone. From being chatty, I was a low person again. I couldn't cope. I went into hospital again. And that's when I tried to commit suicide.

'I didn't rush into it. I thought about it first. I wrote a note to my family. It said, "Please forgive me. I don't mean to hurt you. I don't blame you. It's just something I can't deal with. I hope you can get on without me." I brought the note in my back pocket. I had thought of leaving it under a pillow, but I worried someone might get it before I got to kill myself. I had been thinking about how I would do it for some time. (I went into the building the disused hospital) and up to the second floor. I remember there was glass littered around. I picked some up and thought, I could slit my wrists. But I thought, no, that would hurt. So I didn't do that. I thought about hanging myself too. Some time before I'd made a kind of noose, but I hadn't even put it round my neck; it had been a crude attempt. Anyway, I wasn't certain it would work. That's why I decided to jump.

'After I'd landed, I was unconscious for a while. But when I came round, I remember hearing the birds singing. The sun was beating down. It was ten or eleven in the morning. I wasn't sure if I was dead or alive for a while. The nurses were looking for me by this stage. I remember hearing one of them calling for me. I tried to lift my arm to call her over, but it was broken. I didn't feel pain, but it didn't feel right. I'd shattered the bones of my heel. I'd broken my front teeth. I felt actually happy to be alive; happy that it didn't work. I remember the nurse putting a blanket over me, but I can't remember the trip to the general hospital. The next thing I remember is going into a tunnel machine for a CT scan. And just before I was pushed in, another uncle, my Uncle Joe, was there. I remember saying "Joe, I'm sorry," and then I was unconscious again.

'That was my turning point. I have been through a lot of shit since then, but I have never been suicidal. People took me seriously now. Nobody did before, not even the doctors. I wrote in my note, as well, that my doctor didn't seem to believe me, and they changed me to another consultant after that. I'm still with the new one; I get on well with him. I watched the 1998 World Cup in hospital. I remember France winning. I couldn't move, and I left the hospital in a wheelchair; it was a while before I walked again.

> ❝ I don't think my doctor believed my story. He didn't believe what I was going through ❞

'In 1999 I went back to college to do the same course as before, mechanical engineering. The doctor had sent a note saying why I'd had two years out. I stayed a year and got my certificate, but by then I'd lost interest. I'm glad I went back; it was a good thing to do, but I haven't done engineering since. After college I did carpentry for a builder. That was something I'd always done growing up. Over the years I'd done jobs for friends.

'In the summer of 2001 I went off to America on a summer working holiday with two friends. That was okay, but I was getting panic attacks. I was still on medication, but I didn't feel I was good enough. I had paranoia too. When I got back, my Uncle Michael, the one who was a Samaritan, suggested that I see a counsellor. I went to one, but the first few times I saw her it was awkward. I found it impossible to describe how I was feeling. I hadn't the words in my head. But she was good. She was a woman of fifty or sixty, and I found her very friendly. In time she did help. She'd get me to draw pictures and analyse what they meant. At the start I drew constricted circles, using just a corner of the paper. She said, "What do you think that means?" I said, "Maybe I don't deserve space or time. Maybe I don't deserve to be happy."

'At this stage I wasn't working full-time. I was on disability allowance. I wasn't getting up every day at seven. When I felt bad I would sleep in. That was my way of dealing with how I felt. The counsellor labelled my panic attacks for me. Being aware of what they were was a great help. She gave me tips on how to cope with them. She helped me to concentrate on good, slow breathing. She made me aware of what was making me panic. She said, "Something must be triggering it." I'd always get them in nightclubs. There was this pushing and pulling feeling, and this pressure in my head. I felt I was being dragged everywhere. I don't get them any more.

'She told me about an organisation called GROW. It's like Alcoholics Anonymous, but for people with a mental illness. The first time I went, I felt kind of awkward. I thought, is this me? They told me not to say anything that first time. They said I wouldn't understand the structure of the group. But they were all friendly. They were welcoming and that was a great help. Some of them were telling their stories. They were not all "good" stories, but they were all honest and open. I thought, Jesus, if these people can be honest, maybe I can as well. That was a help. We could talk one on one too. It gave me hope straight away. After two or three weeks I felt comfortable with the group. I'd get a lift with an older man, and I got close to him. But he had a heart attack and passed away. After that, I stopped going for a while.

'I was playing football at the time, and the training clashed with the meetings. So I was missing the meetings for a good reason.

I missed meetings for about a year and a half. I was working full-time at carpentry, but things were starting to go downhill again. I had taken cocaine and ecstasy; not much, but too much for me. I'd take it every second weekend, when I was about 24 to 26. It wasn't something I was desperate to do, but it was there. I knew it was dangerous for me to do this because a psychiatric nurse had told me so. After a while my mind was gone. I just felt paranoid, and it gradually got worse and worse.

'In 2006, I went missing for a day. I got into my car and deliberately left my phone at home. I told one of my sisters, "I am taking life too seriously." I just drove. I didn't know where I was going even. I ended up in Maynooth. I remembered it from when I'd go up to Dublin doing deliveries with a cousin of mine. I knew it was where they trained priests. I thought, maybe someone there can help me. They know about the meaning of life and religion and that kind of stuff. But when I got there, I thought, I can't burden another man with what I am thinking. How can I? Going back home, I remembered my family and friends. I thought they might be worried. They knew I'd been feeling bad, though not how bad. And they didn't know where I was. They might think I'd driven off a cliff. A week before I had said to my boss, "I can't hack this. My concentration is gone."

'I didn't agree to go back to hospital, but my sister brought me in. I sat in the back seat of the car. She and a nurse were trying to get me out, but my two feet were curling under the front seat. Eventually they dragged me out. I had ECT therapy. I was in there for nine weeks. That's the longest time I was ever in hospital. Since that day, though, I've been relatively free from depression. I get the odd bad day. Awareness is a great thing. I now have all the information and I understand my condition.

'When I came out of hospital, I helped to build a house. We got that done in eighteen months. I'm now doing a start-up course to help me get back into the community. It's giving me the motivation to get up and out, and to get lots of work done during the day. In September I'm going back to college. I'm looking forward to that. I'm on three tablets a day now. They're not an issue. I will take them for as long as I need them. I meet my counsellor once every six months. I know I can always go back to her if I need her.

❝ I went to GROW to get help for myself, but you help other people as well ❞

'I don't have a girlfriend. I've never had a relationship that lasted as long as a year. I've been close to a few girls, but we just drifted apart. I still live in my parents' house, but I now have my own room. They built it on after I had been in hospital the first time. I want to move out eventually, but I would not have been ready for it years ago. I go away a lot, but apart from when I was in the States, I've never experienced living on my own long term.

'I go to GROW every week now. It has helped me a lot. It gave me the confidence to talk about my illness. I don't tell everyone about my depression, but my friends all know now. Nobody looks away and laughs. Nobody could say anything about me that would be as bad as I thought about myself. I am in a strong place now, though. I am happy with myself. I am not on top of the world at all, but I am comfortable. I don't dread the downs now. I used to think, oh here it comes again. Now I think, it will pass if I just let it. I used to feel most alone in crowds. If there were five or six people at a party, I'd feel disconnected from everybody. I feel part of society now.'

❝ People don't understand mental illness. When I was suffering, I thought people were going to attack me. They probably thought I was going to attack them. There is fear on both sides – fear of the unknown ❞

23

The things that helped

Information
- I didn't get any information early on. It really helps when someone explains to you what is wrong and how you can help yourself.

Exercise
- I still play football. I walk too, but probably not enough.

Music
- I like all kinds of music from dance to classical. I like rock and traditional Irish. I listen to music when I am down, to get me up; and I listen to it to keep me good.

Writing
- I haven't written for a while, not since I was in hospital the last time. It helped when I was down. I'd write at night when I should have been asleep. Now I look back on it and I think, 'jeez, that is how far I have come.'

Cognitive Behavioural Therapy
- My doctor recommended this. I had some sessions before I went into hospital the last time, and some after I came out. It helps you to check if your thoughts are becoming negative. It helps you to stop the thoughts. With practice you do that subconsciously.

WRAP (Wellness Recovery Accident Plan)
- That was amazing. You write down all the triggers and all the things that make you feel good. For me that's going for a walk, chatting with friends or writing things down. If you put all those things in place while you are

feeling well, you are more likely to get through the downs. The course kept me grounded.

Keeping contact with people

■ I need to be alone when I am going through a low, but immediately afterwards, if I think a friend is ignoring me, I will go and chat to them. I'll find that everything is normal and not negative at all.

Helping other people

■ I get a great buzz helping my family. And by going to GROW meetings, listening to other people and have them listen to me. I give advice and share my story. I've told it at a seminar. I got a great kick out of that.

Other people's wisdom

■ At my lowest point I got strength from a quote by Winston Churchill, 'If you're going through hell, keep going.'

The things that didn't help

Recreational drugs

■ Smoking hash definitely didn't help. Neither did cocaine nor ecstasy. All those things made my mood and my paranoia much worse. Those things are not looked down on, though, and that is the problem. I get out a lot now and I don't drink. And when at a party, if hash is passed around, I don't have any. I used to think I had to have some, or I'd stand out from the crowd. It was follow the leader. Now I say 'No'.

Self-help books

■ I read a few, but I felt too bogged down. I'd rather talk to people face to face. When you read self-help books, you almost self-diagnose. I don't find that helpful.

Anthony's Advice

1. The time to do something is when you really don't feel like doing it. Whether it's taking exercise or visiting a friend. I got the most benefit from going to meetings when I really didn't want to go.

2. Keep working on yourself when you are okay, because you can't work on yourself when you are down. Put things in place. Discover your triggers. Become self-aware.

3. If something works for you, keep doing it. If it doesn't work, stop.

4. When you are comfortable, you are not learning about yourself. You have to get out of your comfort zone. I don't avoid difficult places like nightclubs. I challenge myself even when I am feeling low. That way you learn about yourself and get onto an upward curve.

FOR MORE INFORMATION:
GROW – www.grow.ie

CHAPTER THREE
Valerie

Valerie Maout, aged forty, suffered from severe post-natal depression after the birth of her twins in 2007. Thanks to help from her local mental health services and from support groups, she is now well on her way to recovery.

Valerie Maout was born and raised in Brittany. After a happy childhood, she stayed in the area to work. In her thirties Valerie was working as a secretary on a newspaper in Rennes when she met Cormac, who was teaching Irish in the city. The two fell in love, and when Cormac had to return home to Cork, Valerie decided that she would live with him there. 'I wanted to follow Cormac wherever he would decide to go, and Cork was his place. We live in Cúil Aodha in the Gaeltacht area; it's half-way between Cork and Tralee. It's a lovely place. His family are still here and I had no qualms about moving here. I thought that since I was a Celt, it would be just like living with my cousins. I thought, they have supermarkets, ATM machines and cinemas; I should be okay there.

'But it was a culture shock. The Irish are not like the French. Everything was different. Not better or worse, just not the same. I was being cut from my roots and the environment I was used to. I'd moved from a place where I had a job, a family and friends, and I was used to living in a big city. You can easily feel isolated here. I struggled for the first year. I found myself in the dark. I couldn't see any light except around me and my partner. I was crying a lot. I went to my GP and said, "I don't want this relationship to be ruined because I am not feeling good," and the GP said, "I think you are going through a little depression." She put me on an antidepressant, and that helped me. But at that same time, we decided to try for a baby. I expected that it would take time, but as soon as I stopped the contraception, I fell pregnant. I managed to wean myself off the antidepressant.

'I had a healthy pregnancy, and our daughter, Neasa, was born in November 2005. She was a blessing, but having a baby was another big culture shock. I got the blues. Within a few months of the birth, I wasn't feeling comfortable with myself or with my life.

I've always been a good sleeper. When I feel low, I want to lie on the ground and just sleep, sleep, sleep. I would escape from life that way. I'd go to bed early and have a nap during the day. It helped me forget about everything. But with a baby that was no longer possible.

'I had rows with Cormac. I felt weepy and not great at all. I did enjoy my baby, but perhaps not as much as I should have. I went to my GP and she put me back on the antidepressants. That helped me. It was a good crutch, and I was then able to keep my head above water. I was looking for help on the internet, and I came across the Post Natal Depression Ireland website. It's run from Cork. I got in touch with Madge Fogarty, who runs the group, and I went to their meetings. They're held once a month in Cork Hospital. You just talk about what you are going through. A lot of mums go through post-natal depression, and some don't need to go on medication. I believe in the power of talk. It's a chance to say, "Life is not great. This is what I am feeling." Some mums only need one or two sessions. I needed more, but I found the group excellent.

'I got through the depression within six months, but we wanted another baby. I'd started medication in April 2006; I stopped taking it in December. By February 2007 I was pregnant again. And then during a scan, I discovered I was having twins. It was, Oh my God, but I was thrilled. I have always wanted to have twins, so for me it was a dream come true. Cormac was abroad on business at the time. He runs his own translation company, translating from English to Irish. I called him and said, "Well, there is a surprise. There are two." He said, "That is the best news ever." He was really happy.

'My pregnancy was good until the end when they found out that one of the twins wasn't growing very well. I was put under observation, and when I was thirty-four weeks' pregnant the doctors decided they would deliver the babies by C-section. The best time for twins to be born is between thirty-seven and thirty-eight weeks. It's not good if they are born before thirty-three weeks, so I was relieved to have lasted that long. And they were fine. But having premature babies is never easy. When I say to people that my babies were six weeks premature they say, "Oh, that's okay." But no, it isn't!

'People underestimate the problems women go through. Thanks to the progress of medicine, premature babies have a much better chance of survival, but it is so stressful for the parents. One of my babies spent one week in the neo-natal unit, and the other spent two weeks, so I went home with just one twin. I had to tear myself between the two. We lived an hour away from the hospital, and I couldn't drive because of the C-section. I had to rely on people to take me to the hospital for a quick feed and take me home again. And you can hardly hold the babies when they are in an incubator. You hear all these beeps. It is not a friendly environment. It was tough.

'It was very hard for those first three months. I was getting no sleep because the twins had reflux colic. I had thought that having had one baby, it would all be better, but it was like starting from scratch again. I would wake around six after a dreadful night where I'd have been up from midnight until four in the morning. I'd have no sleep at all. One of the twins would have been sleeping, but the other one would have been crying. At six the two of them would be asking for another feed. I'd feed them, then make a point of being at breakfast with Neasa. Maybe I was mad. A friend who had one baby after another said she would feed the baby and not leave the bed. Her husband cared for the elder child, but I could not do that. It was

❝ When I had Neasa, I felt as if I had been run over by a bus, but after Lorcán and Étaín had been born, I felt like I'd fallen off a cliff ❞

important to me that she see me at breakfast. Neasa went to a child-minder in the mornings for the first three months.

'In the mornings the twins were good. After their feed at six, they'd sleep for maybe three hours. That was great, but I was stupid. I never took a rest. I'd clean the house and by eleven or midday the twins would start to cry again. They'd be needing a feed. The second half of the day was horrendous. I'd spend my afternoons on the couch in front of the TV, feeding one after the other, or both at once, or holding one who was crying, or walking round the house with one in my arms and one in the buggy.

'My partner did the cooking. He was working from a home office at the time, but it was hard for him too. By six in the evening I'd be exhausted and totally empty with no more milk. The twins would still not be contented, so I'd give them a bottle of formula to complete the feeds. And from eight until ten, midnight or even two in the morning, they would be so colicky with reflux that they wouldn't stop crying. I'm laughing about it now, but I would not wish a scenario like that on my worst enemy. I was trying to keep track of their dirty nappies, but I'd lost control of everything. And, of course, I wouldn't have a shower for three or four days. There never seemed to be time. I was the dirtiest thing!

'I did have help. One of my sisters, Isabelle, came over when the twins were a month old. She could only stay two days; she has three children of her own, but it was a great support. Our mother died more than twenty years ago. When Isabelle had her babies, she missed our mother terribly. She said it was hard not having her there for support. So she made a point of coming to me after Neasa was born as well. She was amazing.

'Cormac's family lived near us. I get on really well with his mother; she is a saint. She would come and spend the nights with us. She would manage both the babies on her own so that I could have some rest. At the time, I was insisting she wake me when the

❝ I remember it was winter, and I would see the lights of his mother's car at ten at night. It would be "Oh yes!" It was such a relief ❞

twins cried, but she ignored me. She was amazing. She'd turn off the baby monitor. She'd feed the twins with expressed breast milk or with formula. I didn't feel good about that, but it was a real help.

'We have a wonderful community here. Because we live in a remote area, where there is no cinema and no nightclub, there is a great sense of community spirit. I had met a lot of people since Neasa was born. Sometimes the house was thronged with people wanting to help us. But we did have days, even weeks, when we saw nobody. It was not something that we could regulate.

'I breastfed for the first three months. It's not the easiest road to take, but it is the best thing to do for the babies. And when your whole world is upside down, it is one thing that you have control over. But people were seeing me exhausted, so they were saying, "Stop breastfeeding. You're putting too much pressure on yourself. You'll have to give them a bottle instead." I stopped at three months, and my first thought was, oh, that is a relief. But afterwards I wondered if I'd done the right thing. I think I made the right decision, but I'm still feeling a little bit guilty about it. Giving a bottle didn't help the reflux colic, and I didn't feel good about that. Maybe I should have carried on; or maybe I should have continued breastfeeding but given a bottle as well.

'I wasn't eating properly. I was eating a lot of comfort food, things like crisps and chocolate. Every time I passed the fridge, I would open it and just gulp something down. I was feeling frustrated and hurt and not good at all. I was trying to fill the emptiness inside, and eating is an easy comfort option. Food is available, reachable and it is not toxic. But I was putting on a lot of weight. I was eating to feel better, but I hated myself.

'I began to feel overwhelmed. It was horrendous. At four months the babies were a bit better. Month by month their reflux improved. At six months we baptised them. I remember that day I felt really bad. I looked good. I managed to dress well in an outfit I'd bought for a wedding. I wore high heels. I made a speech to thank everybody who had helped us through. I remember I cried and made a lot of other people cry too. I put on a smiley face, but I was overwhelmed by my feelings. I just wanted to cry out for help. One of my friends gave me a buffet as her present to the twins. Everyone brought a salad, bread or cheese. They were all wonderful! It was a good day, but I look at those pictures and think, "I was feeling so low. How did I do it?"

❛ I was looking at everyone, thinking, please, please help me. You feel detached. You feel you're the worst person in the world, and you just want to crawl under a duvet ❜

'That whole time is a blur. The babies were not feeding well. They would drink just two or three ounces of formula, and that could take an hour. I was feeding them constantly. I got frustrated, and I would scream at the twins and throw the bottles around the room. Neasa, thank goodness, was wonderful. She loved her baby brother and sister. She was not even two when they were born, but she became a great help. We were very lucky with her.

'Around that time, though, there was a terrible atmosphere in the house. I was having a lot of arguments with Cormac. I wasn't being fair to him, because he was sleep-deprived too. He would help me in the mornings to get the twins up, but if he was not putting on the "right" babygro I would go mad. We were having arguments about tiny things.

'One evening we had a huge row. I stormed out into the car. I'd do that when we had any crisis. I would drive one or two kilometres. Then I would think, where do I go? I'd think, I don't know. I don't know any place to go. So I'd go home. That evening I felt so terrible that I started to attack my face with my nails. When I got home, Cormac didn't say anything about it, but it was quite obvious. And the following day he said, "What did you do to your face?" Everyone noticed, and I said, "Oh, a mosquito bit me." That was my wake-up call.

'A few days later I went to see my GP. She was wonderful. She put me on the antidepressant Lexapro. That was a good crutch. It helped me to raise my head and put things into perspective. She sent me to see a psychiatrist in a Cork hospital for an assessment. The consultant felt I should see a local psychiatrist on a regular basis. I saw her every month at the start, then every three months and now it is every six months. My appointments last for just ten minutes. It's, "Are you well?", "Do you need to increase your dose or are you okay with the drug?"'

Life, though, did not improve. 'Two weeks after visiting the GP, I had another crisis. I was completely overwhelmed. It was like a huge wave, and I wanted to get the pain out. I cut myself. I cut my arm, and afterwards I felt a sense of relief. I felt calmer. I self-harmed over a period of six months, though not very frequently. Cormac knew, and he thought I was crazy. He was afraid to leave me alone. He said "What will you do?" He wasn't sure if maybe I would go further.

'The psychiatrist arranged for a mental health nurse to visit me every week. That was such a great help, because it was really hard going anywhere with the babies. Instead someone came to visit me and she was a wonderful person. She assessed the situation, and she was listening to me and she was never judgemental. When I was telling her about my sad life and weeping about it, she wasn't making me feel that I was the worst. She never made me feel that I was "a mad mother". She was helping me, step by step, through my recovery.

'At first she just listened, but after a while she began to give me tips. She told me to go to bed at ten o'clock. I had got into the habit of staying up late, watching crap TV, and then I would blame myself for feeling so tired the next day. She told me to set three goals for the day. Once I did something I would tick it. I would think, right, I did something with my day today. It made me feel good. But she said that on my bad days when I wasn't feeling so good, I should just take things easy. I should stop doing everything, except, of course, taking care of the children. All those things make sense, but you have to be told to do them.

'The nurse helped me with my diet too. When I admitted to her that I was bingeing, she told me things like, "Take your meal at the table. Make sure you only eat at the table and never in front of the TV." She said that once I had taken something from the fridge, I should immediately put the remains back in the fridge. She said "Don't have food lying around the house."

'I was still going to see Madge Fogarty of Post Natal Depression Ireland and attending the meetings that she organised in Cork. It helped me to put things in perspective. When you hear other people's stories, you think, okay I am not on my own, there are other mums going through it. For some mums, the depression is really dramatic. You think, it's worse for her than for me. As I got better I began to give advice too. I found that funny. I'd come away thinking: well I'm a good advisor. I wish I could take my own advice when I am at home.

'I was also in touch with the Irish Multiple Birth Association. There were support groups in Dublin, but I felt there should also be one in Cork. And when the twins were a year old, in September 2008, I decided that since nobody else was doing anything about it, I would create a group. I contacted the organisation, and they gave me support and technical help. They put me in touch with another mum of twins who lives in Cork. That was good. Together we felt stronger. We set up a group in February 2009. We called it the Cork Multiples Club. We have a coffee morning every month. It's great to get together. There are so many extra issues for mums who have twins. Sleep deprivation is a big thing. There are also issues like sharing, feeding and the problems of just getting out of the house. It's hard to get babysitters too. Few people are keen to look after two babies. Having twins can be isolating.

'Usually we have a speaker. Madge Fogarty came to one meeting to talk about post-natal depression, because that is something that is very common with mums of twins. We've had someone talking about childcare, and the pressure working can put on parents, and we've had a speech therapist. We run a lot of family events, and we're planning to organise a Christmas party too.

'I have created another group here in the village. We meet every two weeks and we just have a coffee and chat. There will be around six of us, sometimes more and sometimes less. I have a lot of friends in Ireland now, thanks to the groups. Once you have children, you do meet people. It creates links.

'I went on seeing the mental health nurse for nine months. Then in January 2009 I told her that I was feeling much better and no longer needed her to call. It was enough for me, but we are still in contact. I'm still on the antidepressants. I am planning to wean myself off them, but I find the thought of that a bit daunting. I am so afraid of going back to where I was.

❛ I know the nurse is available if I need to talk to her. That is a huge comfort ❜

'My life is getting better every day. The twins are growing up. They will be two in a couple of weeks. They are walking more and becoming more and more independent. They have a lot of fights, so they are behaving like healthy brothers and sisters. There is a great bond between them. I enjoy just being with Cormac and my children, just being together, just to go out and push the buggy with Neasa. It's simple, but it's an achievement when we do that. I love watching the children go through all their milestones. I get a great reward from that.

'There is, of course, a lot of pressure with three young children, especially when you are cooking and you have one on your back and another two attached to your legs, but that is what motherhood is made of. Children are there for such a short time, and I love being around for them. At the moment I'm just living day by day. Cormac and I are hoping to get married, and we'd like to buy a house. At the moment we're renting, but just now I feel a big project like that is not for me; I'm not ready for it yet. I'd like to return to work sometime. Between my two pregnancies I worked as a sales assistant in an interior decorating company. As a foreigner, it's difficult to get the work you are used to. You have to compromise.

❛ It's like when you are on a plane and the oxygen mask falls down, and you need to put it on yourself first. You have to feel good in yourself to be able to look after your family ❜

'When I was going through those dark times, I thought that my bond with the twins was okay. I was reading about mothers who walked away from their babies and I thought, well, I didn't reject my babies. I knew I loved them from day one, but feeling better helps you to build a healthy relationship with your child.

'People don't understand about depression. They want to be helpful, but they have no idea what you are going through. It's not useful when they say, "Oh, you have to get out of the house for a walk or a coffee." Your last thought is going out. You want to crawl under the duvet. I've heard from other mums with post-natal depression that visitors come into the house and try and take the baby out of their arms. They'll send you for a nap. They think it's the right thing to do, but most of the time you want to be with your baby. If you're low, you think they're saying, "I can look after your baby better than you can." The best help, for me, was when people brought round hot meals. Or when they came in and did the housework or the laundry. That was brilliant!'

The things that helped

Visits from the mental health nurse

- I wish that kind of help was available for women throughout Ireland, but unfortunately it is not. I was very lucky.

Running the Cork Multiples Club

- It helps me to help others. Running the club is selfish in a way. I do it because I like to be useful. It's very rewarding when someone comes and says to you, 'I really like the group.' I feel good about it. It's a great feeling.

Joining Weight Watchers

- I went on a Weight Watchers diet and lost one and a half stone. That was great and made me feel better. I think it worked because it's a group therapy. I think I'm addicted to groups!

Talking to my family

- Picking up the phone and talking to somebody is a huge help. Being depressed is an isolating experience, because you can't really talk about it. You are ashamed of it, and you know that other people will not understand.

Chatting on the internet

■ My partner gets a bit cross with me because I love going to the computer when everyone is in bed. It's my big pleasure to go into the office, turn on the computer and chat to friends. I'm only just starting to do that again, because for a while I didn't have the energy.

Writing letters

■ I love writing letters. My letters are as long as novels. I love emails too. I love that link with people.

The things that didn't help

Self-help books

■ My partner bought me *Down Came the Rain* by Brooke Shields about her experience of post-partum depression. It was a good book, but I didn't really relate to her story. I bought a few books about mothering twins, but actually I didn't have time to read with three children to mind.

Exercise

■ I know that exercise is supposed to be beneficial, but I am not a sports person. I do walk now, and I notice it is good for me, but really, if I could avoid it, I would.

Valerie's Advice

1. Don't be afraid to take antidepressants. Look at them as a crutch to help lift your mood and move you towards recovery.

2. Talk to someone. Join a group, see a counsellor or talk to a friend. Talk is vital.

3. The days when the 'black dog' is around, take things easy. Restrict your chores and don't attempt anything challenging. Instead, watch a movie, read a magazine or play with the children. It will pass.

FOR MORE INFORMATION:

Post Natal Depression Ireland – www.pnd.ie

The Irish Multiple Birth Association – www.imba.ie

CHAPTER FOUR
Luke

Luke* is thirty-six and lives near Galway City. His career in finance has been a resounding success. Yet from the time he came out at twenty-five, Luke has battled with crippling depression.

*name has been changed

Today, Luke is content. He describes himself as happy ninety per cent of the time and sad ten per cent of the time. And that is a huge improvement. For the past ten years he's been suffering badly from depression. At his worst, Luke attempted suicide. Yet most of his friends would see him as a carefree clown.

'I had a very traditional Irish childhood,' he says, when we meet for lunch in the garden of a hotel. 'My parents had been married for fifty-two years when my mum died. There were six of us. We were good Catholics. I was sporty at school. It was an idyllic childhood – it really was. When we tried to explore in counselling if there was anything bad in my background, if anything happened when I small, there really was nothing. My parents were enlightened. They were strong Catholics, but they were never condemning. I remember when I was quite young, a neighbour died of AIDS. He used to walk down the street, and my mother would knock us down in her hurry to hug him. All the women wanted to be close to him. They didn't judge him. It was the same when a teenager was having a baby. There was no condemnation at all.

'We went to a mixed primary school. That was good. At senior school, I noticed the boys who came from single-sex schools weren't mixing. They were really tense around girls. I would be sitting in the library with two blokes and three girls, and other guys would be surprised at my ease with them. I fancied girls. I went out with one or two of them. I had plenty of offers but I always put myself down. I said "I'm fat," or "I'm ugly." I made sure people knew that I felt unattractive. In my late teens I was ragged about being gay, but it never occurred to me that I was. There were men in my life I admired. I aspired to be like them or to look like them. It's only now that I realise that I fancied them.

❝ I didn't know that I was gay. I played Gaelic football and I was comfortable around girls ❞

'Besides, until I was eighteen or nineteen, I didn't know anyone who was gay. Then I went to college in UCC [University College Cork], where there was a gay and lesbian society. I thought, that is great. It doesn't bother me, but it still didn't tap into me. I had sex with girls, but it was always drunken sex. I never had sober sex at all. And when I was around twenty-one or twenty-two, I stopped having sex with girls and began to have sex with men. Even then, though, I didn't consider myself gay. I was able to "do it" and leave and not consider it whatsoever. I'd be out with my friends. There was a huge group of us from school; I still hung around with fifteen of the guys I'd played Gaelic football with and ten of the girls. Then there'd be their partners and girlfriends. At midnight I'd say, "I'm tired. I've had too much to drink." I'd leave and go to a gay bar.

'Work was going brilliantly. It was my outlet. I studied economics and politics at college and I did well at that. People always referred to me as an overachiever. I was a perfectionist. But I was having health problems. I'd always been manic about taking exercise. As well as playing football, I played tennis and I swam for a club. I was a lifeguard. I had two back operations around that time, and I was in and out of my GP's surgery with back and lung problems. I really like my GP. He's known me since I was a child, and he has been consistently good to me. He was always asking me about myself, as if he was trying to get something out of me. One day I thought of telling him that I was gay, but then I chickened out. He turned to me and said, "What do you see when you look in the mirror?" I said, "I don't feel good. I don't like the way I am." He went on pushing me, and finally I said, "It's because I'm gay." Then he gave me a big hug. He said, "I am not qualified to deal with this," and he referred me to a counsellor. In the second session the counsellor burst into tears. I was horrified. Looking back, I'm convinced that he was gay but had not yet come out. I went back to my GP and said, "Is it okay for a counsellor to cry?" He then sent me to a brilliant psychotherapist and counsellor, whom I have been seeing ever since.

'It had taken ages for me to admit that I might be gay; but once I'd told my GP, it was instant. I just knew. I started to tell people about six months later. I told my best friend first. We were at a stag party in Scotland, and

❛ From the moment I had told my GP I was gay, there was no more grappling and wondering whether I was or was not. But for that first while I had no intention of telling my parents or anyone else ❜

I told him that I wasn't happy and that I had been seeing a counsellor. I didn't want to tell him anything else, but he took me to a pub where they sold only whiskey. Just the two of us were there. Over the first whiskey he asked, "Why are you going to the counsellor?" I said, "Because I don't like the way I am." He said, "But why don't you?" I went on analysing and explaining and saying, "This thing happened." After a few more whiskeys he said, "Just tell me. Just say it. It's fine." So I went, "I'm gay." Then I erupted in tears. I was inconsolable, and he was hugging me. Everyone in the pub was staring at us. That was the biggest time. It was the first time I had told a non-professional.

'The next step was telling my elder brother. I was moving out of home at the time, and he lent me the deposit for my house. Things got a bit mad then. I started manifesting in my head how people would react. In retrospect, there was no reaction, but I thought if my brother found out I was gay after he had given me the deposit, he would think I had duped him and would want it back. I overanalysed everything. I spent a year telling my friends. I felt all my close friends had to know, but I was putting pressure on myself. Telling people became the biggest drama ever. I told them one by one. One of the biggest shocks was how well people reacted. It was never an issue with any of them. I don't know of anyone who broke my confidence. I was surprised. I'd thought it the ultimate stigma, but people, it seems, don't gossip if they know and like you.

'I told my parents the following February. When I told my mother, she was sitting on the bed. I thought she'd go mental. I was roaring crying, but she didn't shed a tear. I don't really remember the conversation, but I remember her saying, "I'll tell your father." Afterwards, I felt that in some way she already knew. She told Dad the next morning. I saw him at the dinner table with red eyes. He tried to say, "Mum told me the news," and I interrupted and said, "Look, it's no problem." He accepted it quietly and to this day is good about it. But it wasn't brought up again, except when I tried to get a reaction. I'd say, "I met this fellow," and Mum would go, "Oh Jesus, Mary and Joseph." She was okay as long as she didn't hear about it. But, as one of my brothers likes to say, she didn't want to hear about his sex life either.

❬ He said, "I don't mind if one of my children is gay, but I always assumed that I would know. It was the shock. You played football." ❭

'A year after my mother died, my father was singing her praises. He said she was broad-minded; that she'd been okay when my brother got divorced and had a baby outside marriage. He said, "She was a great woman. She never judged anyone." I said, "Yes and she was okay with me coming out," and he went, "Yeah," and he just laughed. He said, "She didn't really believe you. She always thought you'd made a mistake and would come around eventually." I went off the deep end. I was really close to my mother. Really, really close. I realised she must have been suppressing it, because the day I told her, I'm convinced she already knew. So why did she think I had it wrong? Was it just that she wanted me to have it wrong? How could I discuss that with her when she was six feet under?

'I was in a terrible dark place at that stage. My GP had put me on antidepressants; he gave me Effexor and that helped. I was going to the counsellor as well through all that time. With counselling, you get worse before you get better. I used to blame my counsellor for making me depressed, because I was having trouble admitting that there could be any valid reason for the way I felt. We were going through all these issues from my past, when I didn't feel I had any. After a while, though, I started remembering things; how in my teens I had been hiding in the wardrobe or going for five-hour walks. I had built steel walls around myself for twenty-five years and now they were breaking down.

'In my early twenties I lied to everyone; I lied about where I was going. My GAA friends thought I was going out with the swimming crowd, and the swimming crowd thought I was with my GAA friends. My parents thought that none of my friends were going out that night; they thought that was why I was staying in. Nobody could ever pin me down. I was denying a part of who I was.

'I'd thought that finding my identity would make me happy. I thought, I have come out and I have told everyone, so why am I still depressed? What the hell is going on now? There was a period where I understood, intensely, the wider societal issues of being gay. I'd see a heterosexual couple walking down the street holding hands. I was always being bombarded with straight ideology, and it really got to me.

❛ Through it all, though, I kept my sense of humour. I'd think, you're a lifeguard. What is the point of jumping in the river when you're just going to swim to the bank again? ❜

'I went to work. I did the best job that I could; I came home and I went to parties. Everyone thought I was fine, but I was going mad. I'd find myself beside the river at one o'clock at night after an evening in a gay bar. I felt that I was unattractive and that nobody wanted to be with me. Three hours later I would still be staring into the river. So I decided I'd take an overdose. I'd sit on my bed, drunk, shaking and crying. But there was always a reason not to end my life. Someone in the family was about to sit an exam or have a birthday. I thought, if I do it today I'll ruin things for them. That was what stopped me.

'There were times, though, when I was convinced my family would not miss me. A brother's wife said that he was up the walls with worry about me. She said, "He always worries about where you are and how you are. If he doesn't get a call from you, he becomes demented." Hearing that made me worse, because in my mind the most damaging thing you can do is affect somebody else. If I was dead, he would grieve for me, but would soon get over me. But if I was alive, he would always worry about me, and I would continue to affect his happiness.

'I had huge regrets at that time. I felt that I had wasted my life. I'd gone to school, to college; I'd got a wonderful job in a bank. I'd done everything that was expected of me, but maybe it was not what I had wanted. I'm a creative person. I was always good at English at school. If you can be destructive to your own life, I felt that I was. It seemed I'd done everything I could to hijack it. I read economics at college instead of the Arts and English; I played Gaelic football instead of singing. And when I was depressed, I gave up anything that might make me happy. I gave up singing in a choir. When you have depression, you do tend to wallow in it.

'When I was thirty, I took a year off to travel the world. I was determined to get out of the rat race. I went to Australia to work, but the minute I got there I realised that I didn't actually want to work at all. I wanted to do nothing. So rather than work there for a year and then travel, I decided to travel until my money ran out.

It ran out after five months. And when I got back to Ireland, I returned to the same company. And that is a place I associate with stress and anxiety. Nothing had changed. It's my biggest regret ever that I didn't change careers.

'My social life was stagnant too. I've never had a partner. It just hasn't happened for me. My relationships never worked out. And I don't have gay friends either; just lots of acquaintances. If I go to a gay club, everyone will know me, but I still socialise with the same group of friends. I kept thinking that something, or someone, would come along and sweep me off my feet and change my life. But, actually, you have to work at change to make it happen. I'd been away, but everything was just the same. And that's when my life started spiralling out of control.

'I'd been sleeping badly for five years, but I used to lie about that. I'd say I'd slept like a baby when I hadn't. For some reason, sleeping pills felt like the final frontier. And I'd been afraid to have them in the house. But I'd finally asked for them. And one night, when I was thirty-one, I drank too much and took an overdose. I'd tried before; I'd taken one or two, then changed my mind. But this time I meant it. I'd had five years of hell and I couldn't cope any more. I swallowed eight or ten pills, but after five minutes I started getting palpitations. I rang an ambulance and they came and took me to University Hospital, Galway. They didn't even need to pump me out. I remember thinking, I'll take thirty or forty pills next time. They gave me an ECG to check that everything was okay, and they offered me a psychological assessment. I said, "I just want to get home." I was bitterly ashamed, and my sister worked at the hospital. I was scared shitless that she would see me there. I've never told anyone. My counsellor is the only person who knows.

'After that, things started to improve. I wanted to come off my antidepressants. The doctor wouldn't let me, but he did reduce my dose. And six months later my mother died suddenly. It had been a terrible six months. In the same six months I had been screwed over by my boss. I was left sitting at my desk looking at a wall, so I got depressed again. I wanted something to happen to me so that I would die, but it never got so bad that I wanted to kill myself.

'Then, when I was thirty-two, I got a bad chest pain at work, and weakness down one side. They called an ambulance and I was rushed to hospital. I thought I was having a heart attack, but I was kicked out later that night. They said it was just a panic attack. Six months later it happened again. I went to my GP and he sent me to Accident and Emergency for an ECG. I got berated by a nurse for wasting her time. I laid into her and asked to see her superior. I said, "My GP told me to come, and I do not expect to be ridiculed by a nurse." That was a good sign, a sign that I was getting better. I'd taken shit all my life, and when I started getting better, I went to the other extreme. I stopped taking shit. My GP prescribed Lexotan for the anxiety. When I felt an attack coming on, I would take one and the panic would go away very quickly. Now, if I feel panic coming on, I talk to myself.

'In January 2007 I had an epiphany. It was a year and a half after my mother died. I was off my Effexor and everything was going swimmingly. I'd been promoted at work, and though I still got depressed, I understood it. Then, one night, I started crying at something stupid in *EastEnders*. I hadn't cried for a year. Two hours later I was curled up on my bed, still crying. Ultimately, out of exhaustion, I just fell asleep. The next day I went to my counsellor and said, "I believe something inside me left last night." I called it my tumour of depression. He said, "Thank God. That is exactly what we have been waiting for." He said, "I've been hoping that would happen for years." His method seems to be to push and push until you almost reach breakdown. Something bad left, and I have not been depressed since.

'I am now happy in my head, but not in my life. I believe the reason that I don't have a partner is that you have to be happy to attract someone. And I do have more hope now that things will come my way. I want a loving relationship. I want my work life to change too. I still work in finance, but I don't really have an official job. With the recession, we were all asked to reapply for our old jobs. Some of us didn't get them back, but the company can't let us go. So we're sitting around doing nothing. I've done really well there and been promoted five times in eight years, but I'd love to be made redundant.

'I've been out of work with stress for two months out of the last ten. The work doctor agreed that I needed time out. There is a role coming up soon in human resources. I'd see that as a stepping-stone out into the world. I used to have grandiose ideas of owning a huge house, but those have all gone now. If I lost my job, I would rent out my house. Whatever happens, happens.

'I would love to write a book and for it to be successful, but I am afraid of taking the next step. I have five or six paintings that I have never shown to anyone. I wish I had the confidence to show them and maybe sell them, but I'm bitterly afraid of failure. I've never had failure. I'd love my income to come from a lot of different places; I'd love to be a commentator and appear on discussion shows, but I'm scared that if my plans don't work out I will go down again. It's easier to keep things on an even keel and not to mess with the balance. But I am less likely to get depressed than I was three years ago. Three years ago failure would have devastated me.

'There's so much stigma around mental illness, much more than around the gay issue. I never ever had bad reactions about being gay, but I'm lucky. I don't have an effeminate side to me. I don't tell people that I've been depressed. I've probably told eight friends. Ten at the most. I would tell a stranger on a plane, no problem, but not somebody who was connected with my work.

Now that I'm better, though, I'm less afraid to tell people. And of those I have told, a good few were over the past year. I think part of being well into recovery is that I am now able to admit it.

'I like to call my dep-ression my vapour. I think of it as a cloud. In the past, when I felt a little stressed about nothing, the feelings would escalate out of all proportion. I've learned to say, "I know what you are. You are not going to work this time." Generally that holds the feeling at bay. If it doesn't, I'm happy if it only lasts for a day or two. If I get depressed for only a day or two at a time for the rest of my life, I'll be happy with that. I don't need for my depression to be fully gone.'

> ❝ People said to me, "Whatever you do, don't come out in the workplace or your career will be doomed." I came out at work and my career soared ❞

The things that helped

Counselling

■ It was counselling that ultimately got me through. I still see my counsellor once a year. He practises Cognitive Behavioural Therapy also, and he's been amazing. I have friends who have been to him too for different issues, and he has cured everyone.

Drug therapy

■ Antidepressants got me to a place where I could recover, but, for me, it was terribly important to get off them. They saved my life initially and getting off them saved my life ultimately.

Exercise

- Exercise is vital to me. I walk, I swim and I do Pilates.

Getting close to nature

- Some days I would walk along Silver Strand beach outside Galway for hours on end. Or I'd head out to Leenane. That is the most serene place. I'd sit there for hours, feeling at peace. For years I would walk there and not want to come back. Now I find it easier to leave that peace.

Faith

- I have a deep faith. I pray all the time. That is incredibly helpful. I don't go to church any more, because I dislike the rigours of Catholicism. I tested a priest a few years ago by going to confession and saying that I was gay. He refused to absolve my sins because I wouldn't tell him that I wished I wasn't gay. He said I had no right to attend mass.

Writing

- I write everything down that I feel. That has always helped me enormously. I've written reams of poems. When I'd finished with all my gay hang-ups, I wrote a poem about it and gave it to the five people who had helped me through. That was in 2005.

Reading

- I find newspaper articles on people's experiences of depression very useful. And I always read articles by Tony Bates. Certain books have helped me too. *Pulling Your Own Strings* by Dr Wayne Dyer, Harper Torch, 1994; *The Drama of Being a Child* by Alice Miller, Virago, revised edition, 1995. This reads like my life story. It was about being a creative child but never having that side of yourself developed. I adore reading anything by Paolo Coelho too.

Support from friends

■ My best friend tried to talk to me about my depression, but it was clear that he didn't really understand. Another friend, though, was amazing. She had depression too. We went through a phase where we wallowed in each other's depression and were desperate to meet each other. Now we are a huge support to one another.

Massage

■ I found that great as stress relief.

Gaining good body image

■ I've been on a healthy eating plan for six months. I've had terrible body image for the past ten years, and I'm coming out of that. I catch myself looking at myself in the mirror. When I ask a friend how he is, he always says, 'I feel great.' That is my new mantra.

Wearing an elastic wrist-band

■ When my counsellor suggested this, I thought he was mad. But if you twang an elastic band every time you start a cycle of negative thoughts, the pain diverts your attention. It really does work.

The things that didn't help

Drug therapy – when I was less depressed

■ The second time I went on antidepressants, I didn't feel they helped. I felt the effects of them, as if my reactions were slower. I could sit for hours suspended from reality.

I don't think I was clinically depressed that time, just a bit down. I feel drugs were the easy option for my GP. I think you have to be terribly careful when you prescribe them.

Alcohol

■ Alcohol was the one thing that always made me worse. Yet my social life revolved around it. I will always regret that I didn't go off alcohol until after I was over the depression.

Luke's Advice

1. Tell someone you are depressed.

2. Seek professional advice.

3. Take exercise.

4. Write everything down.

5. Don't be too hard on yourself.

6. Keep your sense of humour.

CHAPTER FIVE
Orla

Orla Coffey, twenty-five, is a trainee solicitor who lives with her boyfriend in central Dublin. At eighteen she was diagnosed with multiple sclerosis, an illness made worse by stress.

Orla Coffey is a vivacious young brunette who exudes positivity; she is both attractive and outgoing. Viewed from the outside, her life seems charmed. When her illness is in remission, it is hard to believe that there is anything wrong with her. That in itself can be a problem. 'When I'm on a night out, there is no way you would think there's anything the matter with me. I'll be on the beer. I drink Coors Light and I'll have a few, though I never drink wine or vodka. I love being with my friends, and I'll be full of life. But after a Friday out, I have to rest all weekend. My friends will go to town on Saturday and be out in the evening as well. I haven't the energy. It's the reason I have never lived with my friends. I would hate them to see me like that.' Hiding her illness, though, is a stress in itself; and stress is something that people with multiple sclerosis should try to avoid.

It all started when Orla was fourteen. 'I was an extremely active teenager. I did drama five days a week, and I played basketball and badminton. Then I got glandular fever and had to have six months off school. It recurred when I was fifteen and again at sixteen. At sixteen I was sleeping the whole time. I didn't get a part-time job that year and that is very unlike me. But at sixteen you are not very self-aware. I didn't analyse it; I kind of thought that everyone was like that, that sleeping so much was normal. In fifth year, though, I started to have severe headaches. They got worse. In sixth year, when I attended the Institute of Education in Leeson Street, it was as if someone was stabbing me in the head. Friends would worry about me, but I'd say, "Oh sure, I'm all right." I did go to see my GP though, half-way through that year. He said, "You're in sixth year? You have stress," and he sent me home with no treatment. But I wasn't stressed. I'm a straight "A" student. I'm good at maths and languages and English. I love learning.

'Every day when I got home, I slept. I was in late for class. I'd get in at eleven-thirty instead of eight-thirty. It wasn't a problem. I was missing lessons, but I knew I'd do okay anyway. When it came to the Leaving Certificate exams, though, I felt extremely unwell. Walking into the first exam, I couldn't see. The words on the paper jumped around. I couldn't focus. And I vomited throughout the exam too. I've since learned it was vertigo. I'd go home and then pass out. My parents assumed I had a virus, and I thought the timing was terrible. I'd studied for nine subjects but only got to take seven. I didn't make the last two.

'I woke up a week after the exams and I couldn't see at all. It was as if I'd smeared lots of Vaseline over my eyes. I could tell if a room was light or dark but I could not recognise anyone in the room. It sounds crazy but I went outside. I knew I had to get to the Eye and Ear Hospital. I felt my way to the bus stop and asked a stranger to help me on to the right bus. When I arrived, they thought I had a brain tumour. Loads of doctors came to see me. That time is a blur. I went through three hospitals and ended up seeing a neurologist in Tallaght Hospital. I had an MRI scan and a lumbar puncture, and I got my diagnosis. They said it was a cast-iron case of multiple sclerosis: I had every symptom. When I was told it, I realised that at some level I had known. I'd been getting pins and needles for months. I'd woken in the night and could not move my legs. I'd pinch them and hit them; it took me ages to wake and get going. So the diagnosis, in a way, was a relief. It was good to know that feeling the way I'd been feeling was not "normal".

'My mother took it far worse than I did. She spent four hours picking out a pair of pyjamas for me one day. She just didn't know what to do. I thought, Mum, stop. Calm down, I'll be fine. It sounds crazy, but I loved my time in Tallaght Hospital. I had lots of friends to visit me, and I got loads of presents. We'd have a good laugh. The doctors and nurses would spend their meal breaks with me, and a friend came in at seven-thirty to have breakfast with me every day before he went to work. They gave me a massive dose of steroids while I was there. I blew up and put on a stone and a half in a week, but I didn't care. It cleared up the inflammation in my brain. I could think clearly again, and physically I felt so very much better. I wasn't given any counselling. Nothing like that has ever been suggested, but I read my notes one day and saw that they were keeping an eye on my moods. Every few hours they would write a comment on whether or not I seemed happy.

'I took a year off before college. I trained as a drama teacher, then worked for a while in a bank. I was fine for three months, but after that the headaches came back. I was tired from the commuting, and computers are not good for MS: they put a strain on your eyes. Then my cousin of two and a half died in a cot death. I am very, very close to my cousins. There are twenty-six of us, and I am as close to them as to my three siblings. I lived in Mayo with some of them in the summers for months on end. So that death really hit me. Within a week my whole body shut down and I was back in hospital.

'At nineteen I went to Dublin City University to study business and information systems. I adored it; I loved everything about the course. I'd changed my diet by then and had cut out bad saturated fat. I ate healthily and by second year I had improved my health. During the year I managed well, but the exams caused physical and emotional stress. I am an absolute perfectionist. I never want a two one degree; it has to be a first. And it has to be the best first. I don't compare myself to other people; I just want the best for myself. There were certain exams that I had to do at different times because illness got in the way, but I achieved a first, and I felt "phew". Had I not got one, I would have gone mad.

'I'd always assumed I'd have a career in economics, but I worried that being such a male-orientated area, it might not suit me. For a while, after college, I taught drama in schools. My parents suggested I take up primary school teaching. I love kids and I love teaching, but I thought, no way. Teaching isn't something I'd ever have chosen if I hadn't had MS, and I didn't want to compromise. So I decided to study law and become a solicitor. That meant taking the Blackhall exams. There are eight of them. There's loads of work and it's high endurance. My parents were worried I wasn't well enough for it, but I was determined not to give in to my MS. I thought, just because I have MS, I am not going to neglect my career ambitions. So I didn't. But I did neglect the other side of my life. I didn't go on holidays for a couple of years. I was always looking for courses to take, but I hadn't much energy left over. I'd say to my boyfriend of the time, "I can only see you once a week." It didn't put them off though. It seemed to make them more eager.

'At twenty-three, I decided to travel to Vietnam. I'd always thought that travelling was something I could not do; I knew I wouldn't be able to keep up with my friends, but my sister said she would come with me, and she's used to me and my pace of life. The second I got off the plane, my symptoms disappeared. I went from having to sleep at least twelve hours a night and having no energy to doing fourteen-hour treks and a diving course. I did a serious amount of exercise. I was happy; I had no stress. There were no exams going on and I was euphoric that I could do everything. The diet suited me too. It's so healthy, with lots of vegetables and nothing is processed. I thrived in the humidity. It really suited me. I had an amazing time. We stayed for two and a half months, and when we got back to Ireland, I still felt nearly normal. It was brilliant. I thought, how do people wake up and feel like this every morning, and not feel, wow! I felt well and happy and so, so grateful.'

Orla's good health, though, was not to last. Two thousand and seven was her most difficult year to date. 'In February I had my most severe relapse yet. It was the toughest and the quickest. I got such severe vertigo, I can barely describe it. I felt as if I was falling through the bed. It was like being on a rocky boat for weeks. I was so ill. I couldn't see properly; it made me nearly crazy. I was delirious from the shock of it. It was like falling off a cliff. I thought, is this what I'm going to have to live with?

'My parents were away at the time, and they knew I was upset. They sent over a friend who happens to be a consultant psychiatrist and she was really amazing. I was annoyed with my brother at the time. We'd had a row and it really got to me. He didn't take any account of the fact I was so sick. I told her about it, and she said, "Orla, a lot of people would say to you, 'I really admire you; you do so much and you have MS.'" She said, "You think hiding your illness like that is a strength, but actually it is a weakness." She meant that I fight so hard to appear to be normal that I won't ask for help from anyone. If someone asks how I am, I will never say, "Not too good today." If they say, "Will you come out?", I'll say, "No, I'm too busy." I will never admit that I'm too tired.

> **It was then that I really knew what my diagnosis meant. I'd slipped into MS so gradually from fourteen, but this time, I went from being normal to "bang"**

'I hate showing vulnerability. What that means, though, is that, although people know I have MS, they don't factor it in. They don't think that it affects me as much as it does. The words of my psychiatrist friend really helped me. I think of that time as a turning point. Since then, I've been more careful about managing my illness and my stress. I don't want people to feel sorry for me, but I am fighting a really difficult condition. I can't tell you how many people say to me, "You have MS, but you're fine." The psychiatrist had made me realise why that is; it's because I never show my illness to people. I mentioned it to a few friends and they were pleased when I talked about how I felt. They said, "We know when you are sick, but you don't let us help you." They said they'd prefer it if I was more open with them.

'It took me a long, long time to start feeling better. There's nothing worse than feeling trapped in your body. It was a time of intense stress. I was in an awful state emotionally. I was devastated. The limitations of my illness had really hit home. I never took any medication for stress. I would hate to do that. I wasn't offered counselling either, but I didn't feel I needed it. I did, though, get a lot of help from my friends. One of them, Marissa, pointed out that, as a perfectionist, I always put huge pressure on myself. She said, "You always say 'I have to do this exam in March. I have to get the top grade and everything has to be perfect.'" She said that I could do the exam six months later, and okay, that might be a pain, but it would not be the end of the world. She made me realise that by putting such pressure on myself, I was making the goal much harder to attain.

> **❝ Friends don't realise that having a serious illness is a cause of stress. They don't see me as stressed. I have never been asked, "Are you stressed?" ❞**

'When the vertigo began to lift, I thought, where did I last feel well? I took myself away from all the stress and ended up going back to Asia for the holiday of a lifetime. I meant to go for three weeks. I left in May, as soon as my body felt strong enough to fly, and I ended up staying until September. I went to Vietnam, Laos, Cambodia, Thailand and Hong Kong. I met a girl from the American Peace Corps and we just clicked. We did loads of things together. We lived in a temple with monks and in a commune with artists. I went to see a prisoner too, and I am still in touch with him. It was an amazing time.

'Since I came back, I have made some changes in my life. I have accepted that I have MS, and have spoken about it for the Multiple Sclerosis Society of Ireland (MS Ireland). I would never have spoken about it before, certainly not on record. But I am now ready to admit that I have it. I felt a duty as well for the people with MS who are at a more advanced stage and can't show how it is affecting them. I've made more changes to my diet and now eat based on the principles of Chinese traditional medicine. That has made me feel much better.

❛ I had totally shied away from MS Ireland. I hadn't wanted to even contact them, but this year I have told my story on the radio. That acceptance has helped me ❜

'I've tried to be more selective about my friends too. When I was younger, I prided myself on having "millions" of friends. I'd have friends from everything I ever joined, and I felt an obligation to keep up with them all. That is exhausting. I've realised that it is not morally wrong to cut out people from my life. I always spend time with my "core" friends, but there are people in my life who are really negative, and I don't have time for them. I have learned to let go.

❛ Being sick is highly stressful, but stress can make me worse. Being worse makes me more stressed, and that makes me worse still. So it is vital that I learn to manage my stress ❜

'I've been influenced by Dr Phil too, the American television personality, author and former psychologist. He pointed out that having a chronic illness leads to very high stress. He said anyone with a high level of stress needs to try to counterbalance this. He said it's hard dealing with being sick because you are under par. He suggested that when you are well, you should make a checklist of strategies to put in place for when you are not. That made sense to me. I had exams at the end of March this year, and I usually get sick at around that time. I decided I needed a pre-emptive strike. I came off dairy because it does not suit me; I made sure I exercised regularly and I started having regular sessions of acupuncture. That is wonderful for my condition and for stress. And for the first time in years, I did not have a recurrence of MS.'

Today Orla is well. She is doing isometric exercises to build up her muscles in a gentle way. Isometric exercise is a form of resistance training in which the participant uses the muscles of the body to exert a force either against an immovable object or to hold the muscle in a fixed position for a set duration of time. It is good for rehabilitation. 'I have to lose twelve pounds, because, for me, carrying an extra twelve pounds is like a well person carrying an extra four stone. I also need to build up muscle because my illness leads to muscle wastage.'

In summer 2009, Orla passed her final exams and was accepted into the Law Society. It took just three days for her to find an apprenticeship. Life is now hectic, with work, lectures and study. But she's coping really well. 'I feel normal at the moment. It would be easy for me to slip into complacency and think I'm perfect. I'm aware, though, that I have to keep actively managing my stress. I have to remember that there is that underlying weakness there.

'I took myself off the medication in the summer; I felt so bad when I was on it and I feel so well when I'm not on it. I told my consultant in October, and he agreed I could stay off it. He said, "You seem amazingly well to me." He says he'll review the situation in July.

'I don't feel bitter about having MS. I don't think "why me?" Having MS has made me develop the skills to deal with it. It is a continuous process. MS can be devastating at times and exhilarating at times as well. My overwhelming feeling is that I am strong and very positive. I have had to deal with things that other people have not had to deal with. If anything at all hit me in the morning, I am convinced I could deal with it.'

The things that helped

Acupuncture
■ I find acupuncture absolutely amazing. I started having treatment in February 2009, and in April I didn't have my usual relapse. I had my final two exams at that time and expected to be stressed, but I wasn't. It really helped my stress. I don't know how I would live without it. I have treatments every week.

Yoga
■ I do fifty minutes of yoga every single morning. I find that amazing.

Self-help books and CDs
■ Dr Phil's books on stress have been extremely helpful. So has a Paul McKenna CD called *Eliminate Stress*. I listen to that a lot before I go to sleep.

The Multiple Sclerosis Society of Ireland
■ Talking about my illness in an official way helped me to accept that I have it.

Support of friends

- My close friends have been amazing. I could not have got through 2008 without them. I love having stupid, spontaneous fun. My two ex-boyfriends and my current boyfriend have been incredibly supportive. My illness does not drive them away. I think they quite like it when I am needy because they see a softer side of me. Normally I can be a bit dismissive.

Music

- Uplifting music always helps my mood. When I was diagnosed, someone gave me the Destiny's Child 'Survivor' CD. I love it, particularly track 10, *Happy Face*. It always makes me feel fantastic.

Meditation

- Mediation is brilliant for stress I find.

The things that didn't help

The attitude of some doctors

- I saw a locum GP recently about a routine matter. She said, 'I see you have MS, but you are grand.' She didn't know me. She said, 'It doesn't affect you,' and I said, 'Yes, it does. I am 25. I got up today at midday because yesterday I went to the cinema. That has made me exhausted, and I will now go home and sleep for the rest of the day.' She said, 'I do that sometimes.' I said, 'With respect, you are not 25.' She was dismissive and I found that really irritating.

> **❝ Never say, "I know how you feel." How can anyone know? It's presumptuous and annoying ❞**

Internet information
- I don't like to read up about MS. I don't want to worry about the symptoms I don't have. It's enough to deal with the ones I have already.

Writing down feelings
- If I'm low, the very act of writing it down encourages me to be more negative.

The best way for friends to react
- The best thing is to be quietly supportive. The worst is to hound someone. One friend rang ten times a day when I was really sick. I thought, 'I'm so tired. Leave me alone!'

- Never say, 'You are fine.' What do you mean 'I am fine'? I am trapped in my own body and I can't get out.

- It helped when people said, 'It is awful now, but it will get better.' I think acknowledging the illness and showing hope for the future is good. But not hamming it up and saying, 'Soon everything will be perfect.'

Orla's Advice
1. Make time to look after yourself.

2. Surround yourself with positive people.

3. Prioritise the things that really matter in your life.

CHAPTER SIX
Keith

Keith, twenty years old and from County Meath, is a member of the youth advisory panel for Headstrong, the National Centre for Youth Mental Health. Keith suffered badly from depression throughout his teenage years. During that time, four of his friends took their own lives.

At seventeen, Keith was a sad, depressed young man. He had twice tried to commit suicide. Then he attended the funeral of Roisín, one of his friends from school. She had committed suicide. 'I was in fifth year,' he says. 'I was with my friends doing a guard of honour outside the church. Her mother turned round to us all and said, "Don't ever leave this hurt and pain for any mother." And that is when it hit me. I just imagined that it was my mother walking down there. That, for me, was the turning point.'

As a small boy, Keith lived a carefree life. He loved the outdoors, loved having fun. And he particularly loved his Uncle Pat. 'I was very close to him. He was like my big brother. The first time I drove a car, it was his car. I remember he brought this old butcher's car down to my granny's farm, and I was driving that around the field sitting on his knee. He used to bring me off on his motor-bike, and we'd go shooting. The first time I smoked, it was one of his cigarettes.

'Uncle Pat died in 1996 when I was seven. He was twenty-four. I remember the day he died so clearly. I was talking to a friend, watching hurling on a Sunday morning. I remember my aunt coming into the house and getting Mammy. They were gone all day. And me and my brother and sister were brought over to Bridie, our next-door neighbour. Later Mammy came up to my room and she told me that Pat had died; that he got sick, then died. I cried for weeks. I remember on his first anniversary Mammy allowed me to get my ear pierced. She didn't like it, but she let me because Pat had had it done.

'I was very down after Pat died. I changed completely. From being a happy young fellow, I was low all the time. I changed so rapidly over the next weeks that my mother even said it to me. She said I had a different personality, but I couldn't help being sad. I never even went to the funeral, and I should have been able to say goodbye to him. A couple of years after he died, my grandmother told me that Pat had killed himself.

❛ I never got to say goodbye. That was the hardest thing ever ❜

'I never liked school. Primary school wasn't so bad, but I'd do anything to get out of secondary school. I didn't like academic stuff. Me and my best mate messed around. The teachers got to a stage where they didn't mind. They indulged us but, even so, I didn't like being there. I liked being outside. I liked hurling and soccer, shooting out in the fields and fishing. I liked making things; I still do. And I loved hanging out with my mates.

'When I was fourteen or fifteen, I tried to kill myself. I was sad and depressed. I didn't want to be anywhere or do anything. For months I was really, really down, but I didn't tell anyone. I didn't try and get help. Sometimes there was a reason that I felt bad, but at other times I felt sad for no particular reason. One day, I was at home and just didn't want to go on any more. I remember I was out in the shed. I wasn't thinking about anybody else or how they would feel. I was just thinking about me. I decided to slit my wrists. I hadn't planned it. I slit just one and my brother walked in. He didn't tell anyone. I have a scar, but I have a tattoo over it.

'I wanted to leave school in third year after my Junior Certificate, but my mum wouldn't let me. So I didn't. I did fifth and sixth year. It was great craic, but then people started dying. There were five suicides in the school in the space of eighteen months. And there didn't seem to be any reason for it.

'First David killed himself. He was good friends with my brother and he was always down at our house. The next suicide was Jason. He was in the same class as myself when we started school. He was wild. He was just like me. It was hard to tell that there was anything wrong. He smoked cannabis. I smoked it too. All the lads were doing it. We all drank too. It was just what we did.

'When I was seventeen, I tried to kill myself again. I broke up with a girl and I was depressed for months. That wasn't the only reason though. I'd worked for ages so that I could buy a gun dog. And I got one; a cocker-spaniel I called Hutch. I told him stuff that nobody else knew. He'd just sit there and listen. He was only about six months old when he was killed. He died at around the same time I broke up with the girl. I bought 24 Nurofen tablets. I started taking them, but I got dizzy and after that I got sick. So I stopped taking them. I was at school at the time and someone saw me being sick. He told my brother. My brother then confronted me, but I told him I just didn't feel well. He seemed to accept that.

'But my mother found out, and she asked me straight out. I told her I'd been taking an overdose because I was really sad, and she was shocked and upset. It was her brother who had died, and she had tried to get him help. And to turn round and see that her son was thinking about killing himself too; I know that she was very worried. It was then that she got me help.

'First a woman came into school to talk to me. I hated talking to her. You'd go in happy and you would come out depressed. I went to her for a few weeks, but it didn't do me any good. I didn't see the point. Then I started going to a psychotherapist in Navan called Dr Alan Dibble. I've been going there ever since. He is sound. He's American and I like Americans. He is very understanding and easy to talk to. It wasn't just telling him your problems; just going to see him takes your mind off bad things. And it really helped. He showed me diagrams about depression. He explained exactly what it was, and how I could cope better. He made me feel normal. But the best thing was that it wasn't just talking about depression. I could go in with my guitar, and that was so good.

'I didn't take antidepressants. I was offered them but I wouldn't take any. Jason was on medication and he still did it; he still committed suicide. I think it is stupid giving someone antidepressant tablets. I think they can bring you down. I don't think they control you in a good way. Alan Dibble didn't say I should take medication and he didn't say I shouldn't. He said it was my choice. And he listened to me. Really, he is cool. Talking to him is like talking to a friend.

> ❝ He said, "Just because you are depressed or unhappy doesn't mean that you are different." ❞

'When Roisín died, I was still in fifth year. I felt so angry. Roisín didn't drink or smoke. She was so good at school. She always had her homework done. She was A1. So why would she kill herself? It just didn't make sense. I realised at her funeral that the pain and hurt you cause isn't worth it. It's so easy to use suicide as a way to get out of every problem, but it isn't the answer. You might be sad and you might owe money or feel that nobody understands you, but in the end, and certainly in ten years' time, you are going to be okay. That funeral changed my thinking.

'There was another death after that, and that made everything seem even more senseless. It unsettled me more. I messed around a lot in sixth year, and in the end I was thrown out of school. A teacher was annoying me, saying I was doing this and that. I called my friend Paddy a bollocks, and the teacher thought I was talking to her. She rang my mother about it. I have a serious temper problem, and I just blew. I told the teacher what I thought of her, and that was it.

'My parents weren't too pissed off with me. The school allowed me back to take my Leaving Certificate Applied, so that was all right. After that I got a job as a plasterer. My father is a plasterer and that is all I know. Alan Dibble was counselling me through all that time. What really helped, though, was that he taught me to believe in myself. When I started going to Alan, he showed me how to think about myself in a positive way. He made me believe, "You are better than this." He let me see that I am worth something.

'There will always be help if you go looking for it. But there is only so much that someone else can do to help you. People can tell you to take off your mask and face all your problems, but they can't take it off for you. You have to do that for yourself. But I told Alan everything that was in my head.

'I learned to express what I was feeling through playing my guitar. If I was feeling bad, I'd just pick it up and strum. It always helped. I was four when I got my first guitar. I play a lot and I also compose songs. That is really important to me. The best songs in the world are written by depressed people. When I started writing, it made me feel good. A lot of the songs are about heaven; not about going to heaven, but about dancing in heaven and about angels.

'Soon after Roisín died, my sister held a fundraiser for Teen-Line Ireland. It's a free listening service for teenagers. My sister has released two CDs and at the launch, €4 from every CD went straight to Teen-Line. We also held a fashion show. That night I sang *Dancing in Heaven* and *Angels*, and it was unbelievable. Celine Knight, the woman who started the site, came up to me and hugged me. She had lost both her son and her grandson to suicide within fifteen months. She was really emotional. Those songs always touch people. Last week I was playing in a pub. I played those songs and people loved it.

'I do have a faith. I go to mass most Sundays. There might be a couple of Sundays I would miss, but I'd always try and go. I believe there is something that takes care of me. I've seen it. I'm still into motorbikes and about two years ago I had an accident. I was messing at the time. There is a lane up the road from me, and it's got a concrete base. I flew up the lane. I was wearing a pair of shorts, a vest and a pair of runners, and I wasn't wearing a helmet.

I came off at about fifty miles an hour, and my head ended up about four inches away from a concrete pillar. Something could have happened so easily and it didn't. I believe something protected me. That's why I believe in angels.

'I did damage to my knee, my shoulder, my elbow and the palm of my hand. That was from the stones. But I was able to climb back onto the motorbike and drive on home. I remember there was blood everywhere. My father was really shocked. He didn't know what had happened. It hasn't put me off riding my motorbike. I still do stunts, and I don't always wear my helmet. If I'm doing tricks in a field, I don't bother with it.

'I still miss my uncle. I feel his presence around me. I've got his name tattooed on my arm with a cross and a rose bush around it. I never wear jumpers, because I want the tattoo to show. One day I was down at his grave with my girlfriend. It started raining, and I said to Pat, "Jesus, tell it to stop raining. I'm cold." And it did stop. Then I said, "Tell it to start raining again," and it did. I couldn't believe it, so I do definitely believe in angels.

> ❝ A lot of people turn round and say, "How can you remember him? You were only seven." It's not about remembering him; it's remembering what I had with him. I'd do anything to get him back ❞

'I've always been seen as a bit wild. I was still mad into sport. I was on a lot of teams. I was on a Meath hurling team and the Athboy team, and when I played soccer I was on a team for that too. But when I felt depressed, I'd go off by myself, so when my friends first learned about it, they didn't believe it. It was, "But you are always mad and always happy." That was because I wore a mask. I felt, Jesus, I don't want anyone to know. And I hated it when my friends started knowing. I hated it, but it was good in a way, because being able to tell them meant that I was overcoming it. And when you talk to people, you tend to get a good reaction. They'll say, "Well done, you have come through."

'I've learned, now, that suicide is not a thing to be messed with. I feel sad and angry about my friends who have died. I wish they had opened up. Suicide wasn't the answer. Now that I see all the damage that is left behind, I am so glad that I never succeeded. I did think at the time that if I killed myself it would hurt my parents, but I didn't really care. After Roisín died, it affected us all. It was so terrible that we wanted to do something positive. I wanted to get involved in the community and to help people who were going through depression.

'A friend opened a drop-in centre. It was okay, but then I got involved in the No Name Club. We wanted to start one in Athboy. We needed somewhere safe to meet, and we liked the idea of the club being somewhere where there was no drink and no drugs allowed. We approached our local councillor, Liz McCormack, and she had a talk with a local businessman. He donated the building. It was brilliant. It's amazing to see these hardy boys walking in off the street. Within four weeks they are best friends with everyone. They really open up. Getting involved in the club has helped me. We've since moved the club into a house.'

Keith was hugely involved in the project. He was an all-Ireland finalist in the No Name Club Host and Hostess of the Year in 2007. He also got the Youth Citizen of the Year Award from the Meath County Council in 2007. Then in 2008 he was Highly Recommended in the Community Project section of the Meath Active Citizen Award. Keith is

❝ The No Name Club means a lot to me. I hate seeing coffins driving up the road. I'll do anything I can to stop that ❞

modest about these achievements, saying simply helping others helps him.

'The best thing that I could do for people was to tell my story. I met Tony Bates of the charity Headstrong, the National Centre for Youth Mental Health. Alan Dibble told me that Tony Bates was giving a talk in Athboy, and before his talk he came down to the No Name Club. From that, I got involved in the charity and I'm now a member of the youth advisory panel. Headstrong is a voice for young people. When old people tell you what you should do and what will work to stop your depression, it often isn't the answer. We know what is going to help us. We can tell the adults. They are asking for our help because they don't understand the way we think. I go to Dublin every week, to the offices of Headstrong. I was up twice last week, because we got a cheque for €5,000 from Dublin Bus. Sometimes I go up to say hello and to show everyone that I am still interested in helping. I gave a talk once at a conference in Trim. There were people from the HSE there. They couldn't believe that we had managed to get a new building for the No Name Club, and in a recession. But the businessman Paddy Kerrigan had said he would donate it, and now we have the house for chilling out in and for playing music.

❝ A lot of adults tell you, "This is good for you," and it mightn't be. Older people have a different way of doing things, different from the way it is done now ❞

'My life is happy now. I love having fun and a bit of craic. I'll try anything. I've had a lot of relationships; I've had a girlfriend for the last two years, but I'm not really a boyfriend-girlfriend person. I'd like to get married eventually and have children, but not for a long time. I never got myself another dog, but I will get one again, definitely. I've been diagnosed with arthritis recently. It's in my spine, and it means I can't do plastering any more. I'm sad to have got it and shocked. But I know I will continue to do sport. I'll do it, even if it causes damage. I'm starting a welding course at the end of the month. I can't wait for it. I've been fixing motorbikes too. And I've been making hurling sticks.

'I'd love eventually to do what Tony Bates is doing, giving talks and helping people. I would love to be involved in the Mental Health Act. I will keep up my involvement in the No Name Club. Maybe we will build another house. And I will always have time for Headstrong. Always.'

The things that helped

Counselling
- But you have to find a counsellor you really get on with. Dr Alan Dibble, a psychologist who works with the HSE in Navan, was amazing. But there is only so much any counsellor can do for you. In the end, you have to do it for yourself.

Composing and playing music
- When I picked up my guitar and started strumming, I got lost in the music. I sang about what I felt. It made me take an honest look at myself. The words rang true, and when I perform the songs, people can hear that truth.

Doing community work
- Getting involved in a project is really helpful. You are doing something to help other people and that helps you.

Religion
- I do have a faith. I believe that there is a higher power and there is something there that takes care of me.

Talking to friends

- Being honest with my friends and telling them about my depression really helped me. I'd tried to hide it for so long and that helps nobody.

Headstrong

- I love being on the Youth Advisory Panel. It's good to share our experiences with the adults.

Keith's Advice

1. Don't hide your depression.

2. Find a counsellor you can really talk to.

3. Keep doing sport.

FOR MORE INFORMATION:
Headstrong – The National Centre for Youth Mental Health.
www.headstrong.ie

No Name Club – A national, voluntary, youth organisation that aims to provide an alternative to the pub culture.
www.nonameclub.ie

Teen-Line Ireland – A listening service for teenagers in distress.
www.teenline.ie

CHAPTER SEVEN
Susan

Susan, forty-eight, is a hairdresser with her own salon near Wicklow Town. Her great sadness is that she never married and has no children. Susan was on antidepressants for sixteen years. Then she decided to face her demons.

It was late in 2006. Susan had been feeling down for some time. She wanted to get away and be by herself for a while, so she spent a week at a health farm in Enniskerry. But she came out feeling even worse. 'I had every massage going, but after that week I had a chest infection and an ear infection. I had to take another week off work to recover. It was crazy! I got over it, but after Christmas I met some friends for coffee. It was St Stephen's Day and everywhere was closed. We ended up drinking coffee in my salon, eating breakfast rolls we had bought from the garage.

'We were chatting about Christmas. My friends are both married with kids; that suddenly got to me. It had been hard too spending Christmas with my sisters and their children. I always appeared happy. I was on antidepressants and they made me numb. On those, I could cope with just about anything. But at that moment something just went in my head. I thought, I can't live like this any more. I decided, then and there, to come off my pills. And I've never taken an antidepressant from that day.

'I had a happy childhood. My parents just lived for their children. I have an elder brother and two younger sisters. At weekends, we'd all pile into the car and head for the mountains. Our house was always full. Our cousins all used to stay, and later, when we went to nightclubs, everyone used to come back to our house. How my parents stuck it I don't know. We'd be drinking tea until all hours. Those were innocent days, and we were never into drugs. I wasn't keen on sport, but I was into horses big time. I'd go to a place in Coyne's Cross, a few miles from Wicklow Town, every Saturday.

'The only traumatic thing in my childhood had been moving to Ireland from England when I was seven. We'd lived in a small village near Aylesbury and we moved to Rathnew. It felt like going from one world to another. The first school I went to there was rough. There was bullying. I was okay. I retaliated and was then made to stand in the corner. The school didn't work for me, so I moved to the convent in Wicklow. I went to the Holy Rosary Primary School and then on to the Dominican Convent.

'At thirteen I turned rebel. I was so bold. I hated school. I did my Inter Cert, but in my last year I started missing school. I started smoking too. I was just very bold, much wilder than my sisters. I said, "Just let me out of school." My mother was great. She said, "If you want to leave school, get a job." So I went for an interview at the Peter Mark hair salon in Bray, and I got the job. I hadn't planned to do hairdressing; it was just the first thing that came up. It was very hard work. Coming from school, I thought: what is going on here? But I absolutely loved it. There were no hairdressers in the family; my dad worked for the ESB and my mum was a housewife. But I loved the creation of hairstyles and everything about hairdressing. My mum and dad said they were happy with me working there if I was. I stayed there for quite a few years. I moved to a salon in Wicklow at one stage, then Peter Mark in Bray asked me back again.

'Life in my early twenties was carefree. It was social. But as the years went on, everyone was getting married and having children. I was in a relationship at that stage, but it was a crazy one. My boyfriend seemed to want to inflict pain on himself. He was clearly disturbed, and I thought I could help him. I took weeks

❝ I remember starting at the Holy Rosary, and a teacher banging me on the side of the head. We were doing multiplication and I had been taught a different way. I remember thinking to myself: I have the right answer, so what difference can it possibly make? But she kept banging me and knocking me, and all these little faces were looking at me ❞

persuading him to go to a doctor, but when he got there, the GP did nothing. He said, "I'm sorry, but all chaps your age go through this," and that was the end of that.

> **❝ The people in Canada were nice. They were friendly and welcoming, but they would over-party, especially at weekends. They'd be stoned, and not in reality at all. I remember a pool party where people couldn't even speak ❞**

'In 1986 my boyfriend and I went to live in Toronto. I spent most of my time there in shock. It was a crazy scene. My boyfriend was in a terrible way. I'd never seen such violence. He'd bang his head off walls. My mother wasn't well at the time. She'd ring, and I wouldn't know what to say. I couldn't tell her about the trauma I was going through. I'd say that everything was wonderful. But, in truth, Canada was Nightmare on Elm Street. My boyfriend and I had made a pact that neither of us would touch drugs. In retrospect, though, I'm wondering if he had taken them and not told me. There was one horrific incident where he completely lost it. Something in me just clicked. I said, "Goodbye world." When we came back to Ireland, the relationship finished. It had to. But there was terrible hurt.

'I bought a house around that time, but I couldn't settle. I was back working at Peter Mark in Bray, and I'd thought I was happy. But one day I woke up thinking: I can't do this for the next twenty years. I was twenty-seven years old. I was single and I suddenly felt trapped. So I packed my bags and headed for England. I ended up in my aunt's house in Scunthorpe. My cousin said, "Let's go to the job centre and see what's in." There was a computer course advertised, and because I wanted to do something, anything different, I took that and did all my exams. Then my brother got married. I came back to Ireland for the wedding, and after that I couldn't settle back in England. I was like a lost soul. I was

❛ I remember chatting to the doctor, and feeling that I really did not want to take the tablets ❜ wandering everywhere and getting nowhere.

'I moved back to Ireland in 1991 and lived with my parents because my house was let. I did mobile hairdressing, going to people's houses for a few years, and that was fine. I thought I was okay, but one night a friend asked me to drop her home after a night out. She said, "Susan, what is wrong with you? I am very worried about you." She said, "Those women in the pub thought you were really funny, and actually you were. But I've never seen you behave like that before. You scared me. I couldn't believe it was you." I hadn't meant to be funny. I hadn't realised that I was. She persuaded me to go to a doctor.

'I saw this junior GP. He said, "Try these tablets." I said, "I really don't want to." He said, "Well, the prescriptions is only for three weeks. Just try." And he handed me the antidepressant Seroxat. I was very sad at the time. And he said that with the pills I'd notice a big change in three weeks. So I just took the tablets. I just did what I was told. And he was right. After three weeks I felt great. I felt human. And from that day I was just taking them. The odd time over the next sixteen years, I'd try to come off them, but I'd start to feel low, so I'd go back on them. And my life became a blur. There was a part of me that was numb.

'In 1996 a friend got married in New York. She said, "Why don't you come over and suss out the city?" Two weeks later I had packed and was gone. I was there for eight months, but while I was there I got quite ill. I hadn't had a period in years, not since that destructive relationship, and suddenly I got a terrible haemorrhage. I saw a gynaecologist there, and when I got home to Ireland, I had a D and C. As I was being checked out afterwards, the gynaecologist, who was a very busy man, muttered, "Thirty-five, and not in a relationship. You should have a hysterectomy." I have never felt so shocked in my life. He might as well have shoved a boot in my face. I was stuck to my chair. I couldn't even speak. My womb, which has never bothered me before, suddenly seemed so important. And this man was planning on removing it? I grabbed my mother who was with me and left. And then the tears came.'

Susan never went back to the gynaecologist. After a while her system naturally regulated and her periods became normal again. In the next ten years, she bought her own business. Fulfilled at work, the rest of her life was extremely low- key. 'I got up every morning, went to work, got home and went to bed. I didn't do much socialising. I'd lost interest in drink. I had the odd meal out with friends. I had the occasional weekend away, and I went on a lot of holidays. I liked walking and swimming, but as soon as I started doing anything on a regular basis, I'd get bored and stop. I tried yoga and stopped. Over the years I went on all kinds of courses.

'I seemed okay to everyone else, but I was numb inside. That's why things didn't bother me. I remember at one stage I went to see a counsellor. She asked me why I was there, and I said, "The most important thing to me would be to have a relationship and get married, like any other girl would. It isn't happening." She didn't give me an answer. I didn't feel any connection with her at all. I think she was just the wrong person for me.

'After I came off my tablets at the very start of 2007, I was fine. Or at least I thought I was. But after about eight weeks I'd get these electric shocks up my arm. I'd think, what is happening to me? I went to see my doctor. He looked at the computer and told me I'd been on the Seroxat for sixteen years. That really shocked me; I'd no idea it had been so long. He said that's why my emotions had started to rise.

'Shortly after I came off the tablets, our family house was broken into. And that is when my anger arrived. We'd all been out. I stopped on the way home for petrol. I asked my parents why the back door was open, and they said, "But it isn't." Then I walked into my bedroom and the whole place had been pulled apart. The burglars had stripped it; there was underwear everywhere. I hadn't realised I'd so many bras. There was really nothing much to take but seemingly women hide jewellery in their underwear drawer and robbers know this.

'I was so angry with the burglars because of the shock it gave my parents, two elderly people. I rang my sisters and said, "You had better get down here quick." I rang the gardaí, then I took off in my car. I was determined to find those robbers. My head just went. If I had been on my tablets still, I probably would have said, "Oh sure, it will be all right." It wouldn't have bothered me, but my head was racing. That's when I realised that I really wasn't okay.

'Three months after I came off the tablets, I had a huge surge of energy. I'd go to bed, tired, but then my mind would take off. I'd think, I've no time for this. I would get up and listen to music. Then, eventually, I would go back to bed and sleep. I'd walk before I went to work to clear my head, but my mind was still racing. I didn't realise what I was actually like, but the girls in the salon were getting upset because they didn't know what was wrong with me. I had to call a meeting and apologise for my behaviour. I said, "I'm going to take a few weeks off to get my head together."

'I booked a cottage in County Wexford in the middle of nowhere. I was desperate to be away from everyone with no noise. And I walked the beaches. I walked and walked and walked. One day I walked to a place where there was slanted limestone. I usually turned back there, but I thought if I went on, I could loop back to the road. Then I realised that I'd have to climb this massive hill to get there. It looked like Mount Everest to me. But I reached the top without even getting out of breath. It was as if someone was pushing me.

'Afterwards I walked into a bookshop in Wexford town, and a Bible fell out in front of me. I bought it. I had never read the Bible before, but I opened it, and it was as if it was talking to me. That started me on a journey of looking at myself. It was: this is Susan. I'm not traditionally religious, but I believe in a higher spirit: God. I believe that you can make your personal journey through that God. I had friends praying for me. The idea of that helped.'

❝ When you have depression, you don't know how you feel. I had to learn how to feel inside ❞

Around this time, Susan came across Father Jim Cogley, a psychotherapist who specialises in intergenerational healing. That is, how the past that is unacknowledged can still influence the present. 'Another counsellor suggested that I see him,' says Susan. 'He took me through the trauma of the relationship I'd had in my twenties. He just cleared all the stuff I'd been carrying during those years and never looked at. I had been in the woods for so many years and never quite realised why. It was like a release.

'I was now facing things instead of running away from them, and I felt myself becoming stronger. I was using positive thinking. When negativity attacks, you get lower and lower. I'd be thinking, you never got what you wanted in life. You never got a husband and you never got children. Everyone else seems to have them but you. But now I started thinking, hang on. I am going to rebut this. These thoughts are doing me no favours. The more I rejected the thoughts and told myself they are not doing me any good, the weaker the thoughts became. I learned that I should live in the now. Why was I worrying about tomorrow? Why was I concentrating on next week?

'All our lives we go through change, but I'd felt I was missing out. Depression is what prevented me from going forward. If you start taking tiny steps forward, you will get to a better place in your mind, but if you keep getting low, it stops that transformation. I had been hiding my true self. I continued to read the Bible and I'd watch the God channel. It was teaching me positivity. And I'd talk to my friends; I have fantastic friends. They have seen huge changes in me. They were worried when I first came off the pills. And some days I was still a bag of nerves; I'd be burning up.

'I had dreaded Christmas in 2007. I'd been off the pills for a year. I walked into the salon the Sunday before Christmas. I was down the back, and one of the girls came in and she said, "Susan, I hate Christmas." I just put my arms around her and said, "Don't worry about it." Then I started crying. I couldn't stop. I could not stop crying, so I went for a walk. I thought that would clear me, but it didn't. So I went to the beach at Wicklow and sat there for hours. I tried to write down what I was feeling, but I couldn't. I went home, but everything seemed out of my control. I was in a terrible state. Mum was wrapping presents for the grandchildren. She made some remark, and I went for her. I completely lost my head.

'The following day we were on the way to a Christmas show. My sister drove through a red light and I criticised her driving. A ferocious argument broke out; that wasn't like me. I was normally a peacemaker. They called a family meeting. They didn't tell me; they had it when I was out walking with my sister-in-law. I got home and there they were, all sitting in the house. They told me to return to the doctor; they all insisted on it. He wanted me to go back on the tablets. He said, "Susan, we just want to put you in a happy place." I said, "I want life." I refused the pills, and that was that. But after all that emotion, it was like something bad had left me. It was like a healing.'

Since that Christmas, Susan has gradually become stronger. She says she now feels content about ninety-eight per cent of the time. Six months before we spoke, though, she had another crisis.

'I felt very rattled, and I hadn't done for quite a while. So I rang Father Jim Cogley and drove down to see him. By the time I got to Wexford, I was shaking. My head was pounding and my neck was stiff. I could not believe how bad I felt. He said, "Have you had any extraordinary dreams?" I said, "I have." I told him one I'd had about a bull pushing a girl who was beside me. He said, "What does the bull represent?" and I said "Strength." We talked about the trauma in Canada. I told him about the worst part of it, where my boyfriend smashed the apartment with a baseball bat – he didn't hit me but if he had I think he'd have killed me. I had never really faced that before. I hadn't let myself, so I had never got it out of my system. I had switched that part of me off.

'Going though the whole thing again, the tears just kept coming. Jim said, "I think you should go to the beach now." I did. And I stayed there for two hours. Two days later I could feel this lift; it was like taking off a backpack. Once you start emptying and surrendering to who you are, you start to feel much better.

'A while after that crisis, I remember thinking, everything has gone silent. Nobody rang me; I wasn't getting any texts. I thought, have I been horrible to everyone? But then I thought, no. This felt different. It felt like I needed to be put in a silent place for a while. It was like, this is my quiet time, and when it's over, I will move on again. I was able to accept and to enjoy it.

'Being a hairdresser can be a bit like being a counsellor. You listen to people who are in an awful state. I always say to the girls, "When people walk in here, you just don't know what is going on in their lives." I've heard some extraordinary stories about people going through failures but coming out the other side. Over the years people's energy has affected me; their negative energy could bring me down. When I first came off the pills, if the place was really busy, the energy could make my head really shoot off. Now I have the strength to pull myself up. Now I can help them too.

There's one girl who had been through incredibly traumatic times. Sometimes when she comes in, she is vibrating from head to toe. I say, "Banish the negative thoughts."

'I had thought of doing a psychotherapy course. I have all the papers, but I never filled them in. I feel it is not the time. But I do have a sense of how people are feeling. I know we all hide things, and we eventually need to release them. We all have it within ourselves to release it but maybe some people are not ready to release it yet.'

The things that helped

Intergenerational healing
- Father Jim Cogley helped me so much. He helped put me on the road without taking the tablets that numbed part of me. He helped me to deal with the issues.

Reading
- I read a lot of books on spiritual healing. But I was amazed how relevant the Bible is; it speaks to me.

Angels
- I don't see angels, but I can feel an energy that I can't otherwise explain. I have read books about angels and learned about them from other people's experience. I just ask them for help.

Meeting new people
- I've always been an open person, and I have met some inspiring people. In Killarney recently I met a Canadian Anglican minister. She was tiny and wore a bright green dress. She'd been through terrible trauma as a child and

had been in an orphanage. She's seventy now, and she teaches acting and writes poetry. I found it inspiring that she could come through so much and survive it.

Walking
■ I find walking incredibly positive.

Talking to friends
■ I have some fantastic friends; friends I can say anything to. That helps so much.

Trying new things
■ I've just bought a violin. It's my next project. I'm looking for someone to teach me.

The things that didn't help

Antidepressants
■ The pills helped me to get through my life, but they made me numb. They stopped me from finding out why I felt depressed.

Writing things down
■ I try to write down my feelings sometimes, but it doesn't help me at all.

Susan's Advice
1. Don't stay on medication for years on end.

2. Take exercise; walk away your stress.

3. When you feel really bad, take time out.

CHAPTER EIGHT
Ryan

Ryan,* aged forty-five, from County Clare has suffered from depression for most of his life. But until his breakdown in 2008, this had never been recognised. If he had a problem, it was perceived to be that he drank too much. Ryan had never looked for help. A year on from his crisis, he is well into his recovery.

*name has been changed

Today Ryan feels alive. He's not free from the depression that has dogged him all his life, but he feels able to deal with the downs when they come. He's finally facing his demons. 'I'm taking a diploma in October in social studies,' he tells me when we meet in a pub near a house he is currently painting. 'I want to devote some years to helping other people with mental health issues. I've spent most of my life hating myself. I've had over forty years of hell, and I don't want that buried. If I can help someone else because of what I have been through, I will do so. I would not wish the feelings I have had on anybody.

'I had an extremely dysfunctional childhood,' he says. 'I grew up with intense physical and mental abuse. I was fourth in our family of eight, and that was not a good place to be. I was the dog in the house to be kicked around. My mother was under severe pressure with eight children. She'd been brought up on a farm and had a religious background. The priest would visit two or three times a week. I think the church had a lot to do with some of the values instilled in her; they taught her the importance of a strict discipline. I remember at age three or four getting the stick on a daily basis. I'd be murdered. My nose was put out one time, and I have one open ear lobe and one closed. I was never taken to a doctor. My mother was a dangerous woman, and my father was helpless. He wouldn't say a word.

'When I was at primary school in Shannon, my sister and I would go to the school by bus. She would get the bus home as well, but I had to walk. I'd get home and be scared to go in the door. You might get a "Hello" or it could be a fist in your mouth. I'd be scared to do anything. We'd have supper, then I'd be sent to bed. From eight years of age, I was sent up at six o'clock in the evening. It was, "We don't want you as part of the family. Get upstairs." She'd block out the light with a mattress against the window, and I'd be stuck in there for the night.

'I became a very anxious child. I'd count tiles on the floor, and if the number was uneven, the panic would start. I remember at school, I'd blink all the time, or I'd lick my lips continually. I remember I developed a rash from that at one stage. My mother said, "Stop licking your lips," and she'd hit me. She said, "I'll put boot polish on your lips; that will cure you." One day when I was nine, she called me into the house and said, "Your father forgot his lunch. Take it to him." He was working on a house seven miles away. So I walked the seven miles and I got there and gave him his lunch. I said, "You forgot your lunch." My father looked at me. He was surprised to see me there, but he didn't suggest I hang out or wait until it was time for him to go home. He was in shock and scared of my mother, so he watched me turn round and walk home again.

'One time I was in the school play. We won a competition and the next day we were putting on our production for the town. I was really excited. But my mother said I'd done something wrong. She said, "Go to bed. You're not going to the play." I got A's at school, but I never got praise. I was going through pure mental torture. I was so scared of my mother, that I never told anyone what was going on. Besides I had no self-worth. I thought: I am evil, I am a mistake, I should not be here, so I must take what comes.

'We moved house when I was ten. Shortly after that my father left. I can't blame him. I had seen him being physically attacked, but he wouldn't answer back. A few years before he left, we were all told that we should no longer speak to him. My father lived in the house for two or three years without any of his family talking to him. The day he left, we watched him get into the car. And my mother got a tin full of photographs, and she cut my father's head out of every single one of them. When he'd gone, she turned to me and said, "If you thought you had it hard when he was here, you have seen nothing yet."

'A week later I tied a rope over a timber shed. I put the other end round my neck, but I couldn't take it further. I was desperate to get out of my situation, but I didn't have the courage. I played with killing myself a few times over the years. I'd test myself to see how far I would go.

'At twelve it was time for secondary school. I went to a college in Ennis called St Leonard's. We had a garden in the new house. We'd go home, change our clothes and start digging for vegetables. I'd sit down first to do my homework, but I'd be five minutes into it when my mother would knock on the window. She'd say, "Get down that garden." My schoolwork suffered. I went from A's, to sitting in the back of the class doing nothing. I failed everything that year. I just gave up on life.

'I was in the depths of depression, but I was afraid to let it show. I remember looking around at all my friends and they were all happy. It was, "See you on Saturday or Sunday," and "Let's play football." I wasn't allowed out at weekends. One Saturday two friends cycled out to see me. My mother answered the door and said, "Who are you?" She called me and said, "Who are they at the door? Don't you bring your friends here," and she was beating me in front of them. She said to them, "Go away, or I'll call the gardaí."

'The next year I repeated first year at a different school. By this stage I'd started smoking and I was a bit wild too. And life at home got worse. There were worse beatings. We'd be sitting down at night-time and my mother would point at me and say, "Look at him. Look at the badness coming out through him." She'd say to me, "Get out!" I remember the frustration and the anger. I'd beat myself on my face at night. Then I started climbing out of the window. I'd walk to the village a mile away. I'd hang out with a few of the lads outside Kenny's shop, and when they went home, I'd spend an hour or two just sitting on a wall. I'd go out at ten at night and get back at two or even three in the morning. It was my little escape, my piece of normality. Home had become a prison.

'I went out of the window one night and came back to find the window locked. I didn't care. It was an excuse to leave home. By this time my elder brother had already moved out. He'd had a row with my mother, and she'd locked him out too. He was sixteen. I was fourteen when I left, and I left school then as well. I went into the village and slept in cars; I slept in friends' houses and I slept rough. I had my sleeping bag and it didn't bother me to sleep in a field. I'd hang out on the corner, and I used to get dinner from the woman who owned the pub. I ended up working for her in the bar. I came out one night and my mother was parked outside the door waiting to collect my sister from the bus. She looked straight ahead as if I wasn't there.

'By this stage I'd been to the garda station in Limerick. I'd been advised to by a parent of one of my friends. I thumbed a lift, walked in and told my story. They said, "You are not of age. Go home." I met the local garda in the village one day, and he said, "Would you not go back if I arrange it?" We drove out. He left me in the car, went in and talked to my mother, then came out. He didn't say anything. We just drove back to the village. That garda was very good to me. He said to me one day, "You know you are supposed to be in care until you are eighteen?" He could have enforced that, but he didn't. Perhaps he felt it was easier to keep an eye on me when I worked in the bar. At least then he knew where I was.

'The garda came to the pub one night and told me that my father had come home. He drove me up to see him. I remember running in and giving my father the biggest hug ever. I stayed in the house that night, and everything seemed to be fine. After a couple of days, the decision was made that my father would go to New York, and that my elder sister and I would go with him. Before we went, there was another row, and the three of us got chucked out of the house. I was fifteen when we left for New York. I took a plastic bag with two pairs of jeans and a T-shirt.

'We stayed with an aunt for a month, then we moved into a one-bedroom apartment in the city. My sister and I slept in one corner of the kitchen. My father worked as a bartender. I did nothing. Nobody suggested that I should go to school. After a couple of months my sister said she could take no more. She wanted to go home. Within a couple of weeks she was packed off and gone, and I was left there sleeping on the kitchen floor alone. I cried for days. It was heartbreaking. I was away from everything I knew; the only reason I had gone to New York was because my sister was going. Eventually I got a job stacking shelves in a supermarket.

'It was the early eighties, and after I'd been in New York a year or two, a lot of Irish people were appearing, signing up in the Bronx. I left my father and went up there, starting work in the construction business. I was making a good wage. I could afford good clothes and on Friday nights it was, "Let's go out. We'll drink around the clock." I went to dances, doing things every young person wants to do. But I'd start drinking on a Friday night and not stop until Sunday night. I was deeply disturbed, but I wasn't telling anyone. When I felt really bad, I'd go away by myself for a couple of days. And I'd drink in places where I knew no one.

'I left the Bronx one day, and I never went back. I went to Florida for a while and then to New Jersey. By that time I was living with an American girl and eventually we got married. I was twenty-one. I was convinced that we were going to be happy. I started a company restoring houses. It went

❛ I'd notice the Irish girls having the time of their lives. They thought life was great. I couldn't tell them my story, so I felt misplaced ❜

well. We had a son and we took him to Ireland, the first time I'd been back in ten years. My baby sister was now going to secondary school. My mother behaved as if nothing bad had ever happened. We went back to New York after Christmas, but flew back to Ireland for the New Year on a whim. I was making good money.

'We had a second son, then my depression came back big time. It was the early nineties and there was a recession in America. I closed my company but kept working for other companies. I worked in the evenings doing sales, using work as an escape. I was neglecting my family. Then I found out that my wife was having an affair. She moved in with her boyfriend. We shared custody of the kids, but we had fights. Some days the kids would not be there for me, and other days I wouldn't go to collect them. It was a volatile situation.

'I was in Jersey City one night, in a pub drinking beer. I remember walking through the city, at least I half-remember it. I know that I was crying. I ended up down by the train station, and I think my intention was to throw myself in front of a train. A cop found me, and before I knew it I was restrained and in an ambulance. I ended up in a psychiatric hospital in Jersey City. They said it was for my own safety. I didn't open up. I was ashamed of my background, so I just said I had split up from my wife. They said, "It would be a good idea to quit drinking." And they rang my brother, who by then was living in New York, and he visited me. I stayed in hospital for two or three days. They told me I should see a counsellor. But I didn't. Why would I? I thought I had no value.

'For nine weeks I stayed off drink, then I hit the bottle again. I never had a physical dependence on alcohol. I used it as a crutch, but I was doing myself no favours. I sank into the depths of depression, and I got to the stage where I could no longer work. I'd sleep all day and go to the pub at night. I wasn't seeing my sons any more. My wife was in the process of getting remarried, and our relationship was total poison. Something had to give.

'A friend had a job in Holland with an Irish company which had an agency there. He gave me the number, and I got an interview in

❛ I was a quiet person, but after three or four beers I felt confident. It was such a great feeling. I thought, I feel alive. I'm not going to give this up ❜

Dublin on a Friday. By the Sunday evening I was on a plane for Holland. I didn't know a soul, but I loved the job, and enjoyed living in The Hague. There was an Irish pub there, where all the lads from the company drank. I went out to Holland with a hundred dollars in my pocket. Within two years of working in the building trade, I had enough money to lease that bar. Life was good. At one stage I did get a depression, but I took a week off and hopped on a train. If things were really bad, I would self-medicate with alcohol. I was making good money. I toured around. I went to Australia with friends for a month. I went to this island in Indonesia, and I went to Spain for the weekend. Things were going nicely.

'Then my father died. He left me $31,000 but left nothing to my siblings or my mother. That made me feel uncomfortable. My siblings didn't want to share the money; I then planned on giving a third to each of my sons and a third to my mother. But I heard through the family that she was complaining about me, and I ended up giving my mother the lot. I drove home to Ireland that year in my

❛ I didn't do it for the money; it was to prove to people that I was worth something ❜

BMW. That Christmas was the first time in fifteen years that all eight of us siblings were under the same roof. It was a special occasion for us. I handed my mother the money, but she didn't say a thing. She didn't even thank me.

'Meanwhile, the building crews were leaving Holland. This was 1999, and the economy in Ireland was going well. I thought, this is my time to make the break. My customers were all coming home. I worked for Intel in County Kildare for a while and that was great. I'd finish work at midday on a Saturday and drive down to Clare. I was getting on great with my mother. I was working on the family house every weekend, doing improvements. I put new windows in. I wanted her approval so badly. There was a push to get the house done. One of my sisters was getting married, and the whole family was coming back for the wedding. My mother rang me a few days before the wedding, saying, "The house is full; you can stay in a hotel." I can't tell you what that did to my self-esteem. I thought, how many times do you want to twist a knife in my back?

'After a while I decided to settle near Ennis. They were building new apartments, and I bought one. I started going there every weekend. Then I left Intel and started a construction company in Clare. That was going great. I still had my downs but I managed them. I enjoyed having a place of my own. I was proud of it and liked my independence. Then an uncle died, my father's brother, and three sisters and I decided to go to the funeral. This didn't go down well with my mother; she hadn't wanted us in contact with the family. And when a brother came home from the States, and I went to meet him at the airport, my mother was there too. She said to me, "Don't think you are coming back to my house; you humiliated me by going to that funeral." That was the last time I have seen or spoken to her. And that was three and a half years ago.

'After that I entered a severe depression. I stopped enjoying my own place. I wouldn't let anyone in. I stopped using my bedroom. I'd go to sleep on the couch with the TV on. I stopped cooking too. I'd order in a Dominos pizza, or a Chinese. I was working still. I had a few contracts, but as soon as I turned the key in my lock, the darkness hit me. After work, I'd walk into the pub. I'd go into the corner, because my anxieties were at me so badly. I couldn't talk to anyone. I'd have two or three pints and think, now you can talk. But it got to the stage when I couldn't bear the thought of going home. I'd stay until two or three. Then it was home to lie on the couch. And I'd get up in the same clothes the next morning.

'I stopped doing laundry. I'd go into Dunnes Stores late when no one was around. I'd buy some jeans and a shirt for the week. I couldn't get into the bedroom any more. I couldn't even find the kitchen. It was stacked with newspapers, rubbish bags and cartons. There was a little pathway from the front door to the couch. I still worked, but I gave up on life. I stopped paying bills. I was creating turmoil.

'For a few months, things were really bad. I'd stay in the house for a couple of days on my own. I wouldn't answer the phone or the door. I'd decided to end my life. I had it organised. I chose a day. I was meant to go to the Galway races, but I didn't go. I went down to the pub, and I looked around, thinking, this is the last time I will see everyone. There was an interesting crowd in that night, and a good music session. And at two in the morning I went home. I thought, this is it. I knew I had to die. I had put it off for too long. I was bawling crying. I sat there with the lights off and smoked twenty fags. I went through a full bottle of whiskey. I went to sleep, woke in the morning, fetched a chair and my chisel and took the door off its hinge. I remember taking the screws out of the door, crying and crying. I was thinking, this is my destiny now. I was there, alone with no food, no cigarettes. I'd get up from the couch, look at the door and get back on the couch again. And before I knew it, two weeks had gone by.

'Every day friends would come and bang on the door or throw stones at the window. I ignored them. One day friends were throwing stones for an hour. I opened the window and said, "I'm fine. Fuck off and leave me alone." The next day my sister was down there, and she was crying. I went to my chair, and said, "Leave me alone for five minutes. There is something I have to do here." But I let her in. That was the first time she'd been in my apartment in three years. She was shocked. I said, "I am breaking down here." She had no idea. She'd thought I was happy. She got me some dinner and cigarettes, and the next day she took me to her GP.

'The doctor talked to me. I said I'd been trying to take my own life and that I was still determined to do it. She said, "You need rest. And I want you to go to the psychiatric hospital." I said, "Not a hope." I was crying. She said, "I want you to go to the hospital and to at least talk to someone." I said I would. I said I'd go the next morning. In my mind I knew I wouldn't be around. I'd pushed myself into the situation where I now had no choice but to kill myself. But the doctor wouldn't let me go home. And half an hour later, I found myself being admitted to the Ennis psychiatric hospital.

'They gave me some medication to calm me down. For the first few days they just assessed me. My sisters visited, and they kept saying, "You have to take it easy, you can't be going to the pub." That frustrated me. I hadn't had a drink in weeks. I felt like saying, "Do you not think I am here because of all the shit that has happened? Do you not think there is a reason?" But I didn't say it.

'The staff in the front line there were wonderful. They don't get enough praise for what they do. There was a male nurse who came in to see me every day. I started to click with him. One day we were out having a smoke, and my whole story came out. He said, "You have severe depression." He said, "With the right medication and the right counselling, you will have a good life." He was an amazing listener. Talking to him was, I think, my turning point

'I was put on the antidepressant Cipramil and also a relaxant called Rivotril. That helped me immensely. I was no longer feeling panic. But while I was there, the suicidal thoughts came back again. When we went for our tea and biscuits at ten in the evening, the nurses would come round with the drug trolley. I'd be sizing it up, working

> ❛ He said, "There is life out there. The hardest thing you have done is to walk through those doors" ❜

out what I could take and how I could jam myself into a bathroom to take it. The thoughts would come, and then go again. I told the staff of my plans, and they were good to me. I had trouble sleeping and they would come and sit with me.

'One night, though, I was feeling that I was breaking down again. I told the trainee who was on duty and he gave me Rivotril, but he didn't have time to sit with me. He was run off his feet. I felt desperate.

'I saw a psychiatrist every couple of days. You get five minutes. You are talking and they are writing. You're not getting any feedback at all. After a month the psychiatrist said, "There is

> ❛ When I said I really needed to talk to someone because I was feeling so bad, the trainee said "Think of it this way. When you are lying in the gutter, you look at the stars. The stars will be there for you, ok?" And he walked off ❜

nothing wrong with you. Go home and get your life together. You're going home on Monday." I just fell apart. I thought, what is my diagnosis? Why do I feel this way? What is the story? I got so upset that I rang my sister and said, "I don't

think I can handle going home now. I'm not ready. I want to get better but I'm scared." She organised a meeting with the discharge team. They said I could go to the day hospital in Shannon. So I was released. I went home to find my apartment tidy and clean. And I went to the day hospital and met a social worker.

'People were always implying that it was my drinking that caused the problems. In hospital an addictions counsellor came to see me. She was good. The social worker told me that I now had a choice. I could either see her, or I could meet an addictions counsellor. She said, "Do you need her?" I explained that if I could get rid of my anxieties and depression, I wouldn't need to drink. We made a deal. I said, "If I feel I am going to drink, I'll call you and see the addictions counsellor. Meanwhile I'd rather see you."

'While I'd been in hospital, some volunteers had come in and talked about the Wellness Recovery Action Plan – WRAP. It's the idea of an American, Mary Ann Copeland, and I felt it would suit me. The male nurse had downloaded the plan from the internet for me, and I did the plan with my social worker. It's all about taking control of your life. You work out your triggers and how to counteract them. You also work out all the things that make you feel good. It came together very well for me.

> ❝ My brother rang and said, "Don't worry. This is a small setback." To me, though, it was not a setback at all. Things were falling apart, but this time I was putting my hand up and admitting there was a problem. I was saying, "I am worth it" ❞

'But in November 2008, two months after I had been discharged from hospital, things started breaking down for me again. I called my sisters and went to the GP. She suggested I should go back to the psychiatric hospital, and this time I was glad to go. I was in for just a week. It was good. There was a lot of talking.

'When I left I was still on Cipramil, but it stopped working for me. I saw a psychiatrist every two weeks, but I never saw the same doctor twice. One doctor said, "Try Effexor," but he hadn't taken into account the withdrawal from the other drug. I had the most horrific week of my life. The withdrawal was so bad, that one Sunday I ended up in A & E in Ennis with severe palpitations and sweats. I was blacking out. The dose of Effexor has now been increased, and it's working well for me.

'Since then, life has been going really well. I now appreciate the simple things. On my ideal Saturday, I go to my allotment and take out all the vegetables I need for the week. Then I'll meander around town. And I'll go up to people I know and have a good chat to them; I'll make a point of that. Before I'd just say "Hello" and walk on. I'll go to the pub in the evenings but I'll have orange. I haven't had a drink since July 2008.

'Life is good, but there were all those wasted years. I'm bitter about the past, but I realise that's a waste of emotion. It bothers me that there's still a stigma around depression. It was partly the stigma that stopped me from seeking help. I believed that real men don't have emotional problems. I felt, I couldn't go to psychiatric departments, because people wouldn't talk to me again. I have friends now who pick my brains about depression. They are going through it, but won't take the jump towards getting treatment.

'I now want to help other people. I'd love to start an agency for people who are discharged from psychiatric hospitals. So many of them are discharged to a bed-sit, and there is no follow-up. The agency would contact everyone and make sure they were getting help. That would help prevent them from being admitted again. I was lucky. I had my family onside.'

The things that helped

GROW

- GROW is an organisation that helps people recover from all kinds of mental health problems. I started to go to GROW meetings after my first time in hospital. The first night I got to the door and froze. I walked home again. The following week I went in. The support is really helping me. I go every Monday night without fail, and at our annual get-together, I gave a testimony to the whole group. Their whole approach is excellent.

The WRAP programme

■ It's about taking control and saying you can have responsibility for your own treatment. It's better than just being given pills and told, "Come back in a month." Everybody's programme is different. It helps you to do something positive when you feel anxious. If I feel bad, I will do half an hour's exercise or I'll ring my sister. The programme is good for prevention too. I'm now a facilitator and hope to help spread the course around the country.

My allotment

■ I've always enjoyed gardening, and now I can do it on *my* terms. When the bad days come, and there are still weeks when I feel like staying in bed, I have to go to my allotment or it will overgrow. And no matter how bad I'm feeling, after two or three hours there I'm getting positive again.

Relaxation

■ We had relaxation classes every day in hospital and it really works. When I'm feeling stressed, I will still lie on a rug on the ground and put on a relaxation CD. It helps to use breathing exercises to relax.

Depression websites

■ There was one, www.depnet.com.au, which I found particularly helpful. You could keep a diary on the site and, if you wanted, make this public.

Books

■ *Awareness* by Anthony de Mello, published by Image, 1990.

The things that didn't help

Drink

■ Drink was never my main problem, but I always used it to self-medicate when I felt low.

Caffeine

■ I now avoid caffeine.

People who don't understand

■ People tend to say, 'Snap out of it,' and that doesn't help at all. If you were lying in bed feeling bad and you got a text to say you had won ten million in the lotto, it would not change your mood. Depression doesn't work like that.

Ryan's Advice

1. Don't be afraid to look for help.

2. Take exercise; find something that really interests you.

3. Attend a support group.

FOR MORE INFORMATION:

GROW – www.grow.ie

WRAP – www.workingtogetherforrecovery.co.uk

CHAPTER NINE
Geraldine

Geraldine Wössner, aged thirty-seven, lives a mile up a mountain near Kenmare, County Kerry. She lives a simple, spiritual life, yet she was once an ambitious fashion designer. Geraldine's life changed when in her twenties she suffered such crippling anxiety that the demands of her job became impossible to fulfil.

First Communion was a milestone for Geraldine. Her aunt, a ballroom dancer, made her dress, and it was really glitzy. Geraldine had some sparkly shoes to go with the dress, and she loved them. 'That dress made fashion click for me,' she says. 'I thought, I can be different. I loved the glamour of it. When I was about ten, I started using my mother's sewing machine, and I'd make my own clothes. I developed very much my own style. I'd see something on TV and think, I could make that, and I would. I designed my own confirmation outfit.'

Geraldine is grateful that she discovered her talent so early, because life wasn't easy for the girl brought up in Baldoyle, County Dublin. 'There was a lot of fighting in the household, and that definitely affected me,' she says. 'I felt that I had to keep the rows under control or my parents would split up. I was trying to fix things and to please everyone, and that is a trait I still have today. It's odd that I took on that role, because I am the youngest of three children. I was a perfectionist too. I wasn't brilliant at school, but I tried very hard. I'd get up at six in the morning and go through my spellings over and over again. I was determined to do well.

'When your parents fight, you can't invite friends home, and, anyway, I found it hard to socialise. I was extremely shy. I made friends with our next-door neighbours when we moved in. I was three then, and they moved away when I was six or seven. I was devastated. I felt they were my only friends, and I spent a lot of time on my own feeling upset about it. I wasn't happy at all. But that time spent reflecting on life benefited me in the end. I drew a lot, and that got me interested in art. It opened me up to spirituality too. I'd see fairies in my bedroom. They were my friends. With a child's imagination you do actually see them; now I feel a connection to a nature spirit.

'Secondary school suited me much better. I didn't feel anxious at all. I made two friends in first year, Shirley and Emer, and we are still friends today. I thought the rest of the class found me weird and geeky, but I was talking to an old classmate recently, and she said they thought I was this really cool kid. I always dressed differently and I was in my own world. I was very much into art, and so were Shirley and Emer. We'd paint the sets for all the school plays.

'I didn't spend much time at home. After school, I'd go off to friends' houses and at weekends I was out with my friends from ten in the morning until ten at night. I did feel stressed around the Leaving Certificate. I'd ring Shirley. She would say, "We're going for a walk." We'd have a chat and I'd feel grand. She was always relaxed and that counteracted my panic. My parents split up when I was seventeen. That had always been my biggest fear, but when it happened, I thought, "God, this is better, actually."

'I went to NCAD (The National College of Art and Design), in 1990. Shirley and Emer went there as well. I loved it. If I have any regrets, it's that I didn't have more fun in college. I worked really hard. That first year was a shock. It was tough, because I wasn't the best, as I had been at school. In second year, when I specialised in fashion design, I was one of the best. By then, though, I had decided to aim for a first-class honours degree. I'd do anything in my power to get it, so I threw myself into work, and stopped having a social life.

'The summer after first year, I met my future husband. I was in Greece, on an island called Ios, with Shirley. We had a job in one of those bars where you are supposed to entice the boys in. I met Klaus in the bar on my very first night. He went back to Germany to study, but we kept in contact. It kind of suited me having a long-distance romance. It made it easier to put all my energy into college. On college breaks I would visit Klaus, or he would come and visit me.

'I did get anxious in college though. I'd have deadlines, and I'd stay up all night to get them done. In the middle of the night, I'd break down and think, I can't do this any more. I can't keep this up for ever. But I was happy, because I was doing what I loved. Around Finals time, we put on a fashion show. I worked really hard. My theme was the movie *The Piano*. I had a child model and an extra adult. The child came out first, and you could hear the audience gasp. It really made an impact. My family were so proud and that was great. I was always looking for approval from them and wanting to prove to myself that I had talent. That night was fantastic. It was one of the most magical moments in my life. If I need to cheer myself up, I just think of it, and I smile.

'There was a lot of interest in my collection after the fashion show. I appeared on TV, being interviewed by Terry Wogan on *Wogan's Ireland*. But I moved to Germany because I wanted to be with Klaus. Making it over there was difficult. I couldn't work in fashion, because when I arrived I didn't have the language. Klaus was still living with his parents, and I had my own apartment in Stuttgart. I started off working shifts in a metalwork factory. Once my German had improved, I worked in an auction house and I loved that. If there was an exhibition, I had to chat to the customers and show them where everything was. They sold art, crafts and antique furniture.

'Finally I starting working for a fashion designer, helping her with her pattern work. It was a good experience, but it wasn't really my speciality. So when I saw a job advertised with a knitwear designer in Indonesia, I applied for it and I got it. It rocked my relationship, because I was putting my career first, but I had not been particularly happy in Germany.

'I loved the Indonesian people and learned so much from them. They have a simple attitude to life, and they don't get stressed and angry with people. I admired that so much. It was a turning point for me. But living there was a culture shock too. I arrived at Ramadan, and I had no idea what that was. And there were huge lizards that made weird sounds throughout the night. I found the job tough too. It was extremely hard work. I'd travel from Jakarta to Bogor, which was a two-hour drive. I had to visit all the factories in one day and travel home again at night. They provided a driver, but he drove like a lunatic and my nerves would be in tatters. My boss thought he'd employed a really strong woman who would come in and throw her weight around, but that was not in my personality. It was stressful, and it was tough being without Klaus. Our relationship came to a head. He rang, unhappy with the situation. I stuck it out in Indonesia for seven months, then I resigned and went to Bali, where I spent a month in a resort alone. I just loved that. Then Klaus got his summer holidays, and we travelled together around Asia for a good few months. Afterwards I returned to Ireland, and Klaus went back to college in Germany.

'I got a job in Dublin as a fashion designer. I was thrilled. I felt that at last my career was on track. It was a commercial job. I was designing for Woolworths, Dunnes Stores and C&A. I got to travel to New York and Paris twice a year and to London every week. That was a novelty for the first year, but the job became repetitive, and the travel started to wear me down. I'd come back from New York and have to go to Paris with jet-lag. I'd get home from Paris feeling really worn out. The work was extremely pressurised. If I got a design wrong and it didn't sell, my head was on the line. So I was under a lot of stress for a job that wasn't particularly satisfying.

'After four years, on my visit to New York, I was in Bloomingdale's and I started to feel really weird. I felt sweaty and my heart was beating like crazy. I couldn't breathe and thought that I was going to pass out. I thought, what's going on? I actually thought I was dying. I had a friend who lives in New York. I got a cab to her place and said, "I don't know what is happening to me." She sat me down and said, "You are probably just hungry." After a while I did feel better. I returned to Ireland okay, but it happened again when I was back home. I went to see my doctor and he told me that there was nothing wrong with me.

'The panic attacks started happening more and more often. I found that I just couldn't function. I couldn't do my job, and I ended up handing in my notice. I'd been back to the GP, and he'd tried to persuade me to take antidepressants and relaxants. I didn't want to. I felt instinctively that that was the wrong thing for me to do. I'd never been into any kind of drugs. I didn't take drugs at art school, when almost everyone else did. But the panic got progressively worse.

> **❝ My doctor told me to relax. That really got to me. That is not helpful at all when you are in such a terrible state, because you don't know how to relax ❞**

'After I left work, I needed to claim sickness benefit. The GP sent me to a psychiatrist, but that actually wasn't helpful at all. I went once a month. He'd say, "How are you feeling and how are you coping?" He'd try and persuade me to take medication, and I'd say, "I really don't want to." That was the roughest time. I'd moved back home to live with Dad, and I felt that I had no future. I'd lost myself. I was miserable and out of control. Everything was wrong. I was disillusioned with the fashion industry, and I'd never wanted to do anything else. Without that, I had no purpose in life.

'While I was still in my job, I'd read an article about Holy Island in Scotland. The island is run by Tibetan monks. Two months after I'd left my job, I felt compelled to get there. I travelled to Scotland, even though at the time I found it hard to leave the house. I stayed on Holy Island for a week or two. I meditated with the monks and I worked with them in the garden. It was really great.

❝ I'd sit on the DART and think, Oh God, I'm going to have a panic attack. I got so convinced that I would have one, that I stopped going out ❞

I came home feeling like a completely different person. I felt inspired, but soon I fell back into my rut. I'd sit around watching day-time TV. I realised I had to do something to help myself, and I decided to learn how to meditate properly. I realised it could be a tool to help combat my anxiety.

'I went looking for someone to teach me meditation and relaxation, and I found someone through the Golden Pages. I rang her, and she explained that what she actually taught was Reiki. Reiki is a Japanese technique for stress reduction and relaxation. It's based on the belief that we all have an unseen life-force energy flowing through us. If that energy is low, we are more likely to get sick and feel stressed. When the practitioner heard what I was going through and how severe my stress was, she said, "I think you need to come for a few treatments first." She said that you can't teach someone who was in my state, so that's what I did.

'I had my doubts, though. When she told me what Reiki was, I thought that it didn't sound right for me. It came across as mysterious and spiritual and that seemed alien. On my first session, though, it was as if something huge shifted inside me. I could breath freely for the first time in months. I went for ten sessions. After each one I could feel myself getting stronger and stronger. When I'd finished all the treatments, I was able to learn Reiki. Reiki is not "taught", in the usual sense. It is "transferred" to the student during a Reiki class. It allows the student to tap into an unlimited supply of life-force energy. It sounds weird, but it really works. I ended up doing the three levels up to Reiki Master; that meant that I would be able to treat people. In conjunction with the Reiki, I was learning meditation.

'About six months after I had left work, I was feeling stronger but not strong enough to get another job. I started to volunteer in various places. That was great. I was fund-raising, and I felt I was really contributing. I was meeting people and interacting with the world again. That kept me from being in my own thoughts. It was an important step for me.

'Meanwhile Klaus and I had married. It seemed an important thing to do, but he was back in Germany trying to finish college. He wanted to be a teacher, and in Germany that takes seven years. I didn't want to go back to Germany, so we lived apart for a year after we married. In the end, though, Klaus dropped out of college. He moved to Ireland in 1999. We bought a house in Kerry. That was a compromise. Klaus didn't like Dublin, but he felt that Kerry was somewhere that he could live. The house needed a lot of renovation, and meanwhile we lived in my father's house in Baldoyle. Klaus got a job with a software company, and I was busy taking meditation retreats. It was a good time; we were both engaged with our lives.

> **Reiki is great for anxiety, because it helps get rid of any emotional block. It balances out the energy and makes you more comfortable within yourself. That's important, because when anxiety kicks in, you start to lose a sense of yourself, and you don't feel comfortable in your own body. Reiki helps to reverse that**

'Then I moved to Kerry. I was there by myself for a while, but then Klaus's company decided that he could work from home with a modem, so we were down here together. My mission was to set up a Reiki practice. There were cow-sheds across the way, and I did them up and bought a treatment bed. I put up some posters and people started coming for treatment. I didn't plan it, but my main clients are people who suffer from anxiety and panic attacks.

'I studied and then taught meditation too. I went away on some intense meditation retreats. I was learning a lot about myself and that really helped me. I also did a course in mindfulness in stress management; that was in Manchester, and I found it fantastic. Mindfulness combines meditation with an approach to day-to-day living which is based on a Buddhist principle. It teaches moment by moment relaxed awareness of breathing patterns, bodily sensations, thoughts, emotions and outside influences.

'Mindfulness helped me to live every day in the moment and with awareness. I would meditate every morning and then notice if I started to react badly to everyday stresses. It helped me to make choices in life which would bring me peace. It made me realise, too, that I should stop trying to save the world. I had burnt myself out when I was fund-raising and trying to help people. Mindfulness taught me that the best way I could help the world was to be peaceful in myself. I realised that if I kept my life simple, I would have a subtle effect on other people. My peacefulness could affect all the people I came into contact with.'

How, though, did Klaus react to this dramatic change in his wife? 'I think he struggled with the whole spirituality thing at first. He's relaxed about it all now

❝ When I went on long retreats, Klaus worried. I think he imagined that I would run off and become a Buddhist nun ❞

though. He can see how I have benefited by keeping my life centred.'

But the lifestyle ultimately became too narrowly focused for Geraldine. 'By living that altruistic spiritual life, I neglected the other part of me, the part that loves clothes, pretty things and creativity. And that's when I read the book *The Artist's Way* by Julia Cameron.

'*The Artist's Way* is written as a twelve-week programme aimed at helping you to tap back into your creativity. It does this by providing a series of exercises and tools. For example, Cameron suggests that readers should complete "morning pages". This is where you free-flow write whatever is on your mind as soon as you get up in the morning. She also suggests that readers allocate an artist's day. You pick a day every week and go off, by yourself, to do something that you find enjoyable and inspiring. The book helps you to list all the things that you would love to do, and it gets you to think about the way that you would most like to live. I read the book about four years ago, and I found it truly inspiring. Since then I have done some training on Cameron's methods. I would love to teach those methods to other people.

'Since reading *The Artist's Way*, I have joined a cooperative of artists, and I have started painting. We give exhibitions. I love taking photographs too. I'll go off into the woods and spend a few hours just shooting photographs. I find inspirational quotes to go with the photographs, and I turn them into cards.

'The book inspired me to surf too. It was the one of the things I had listed as something I wanted to try. I saw a chap teaching it on Inch Beach one day and decided to learn. First, though, I had to learn to swim. I just love surfing. That feeling of standing up on a wave and giving yourself to the power of it is just fantastic. At one time I surfed a few times every week. But since a holiday in Morocco, where I surfed every day, I'm doing it less. At the moment I'm surfing every other week. And I always surf on Christmas Day.

'About six years ago I took a course in complementary therapies. The course included diet and nutrition, reflexology and aromatherapy. I loved the aromatherapy, and I decided to focus on skincare. I decided to use a made-up natural face cream and to add essential oils, but I couldn't find a good natural base anywhere; or, at least, not one I could afford. So I began to research skincare and to play around with making my own face cream. After a few years, and with the benefit of some courses that I took in Germany, I eventually came up with a base that has a good consistency. I'm really happy with it. I have a whole range of skincare now. I started selling it at farmers' markets, but now I sell to shops too, and through the internet. My website is www.flourishcosmetics.net

'Three years ago I had a miscarriage. That was really difficult. I didn't know how to grieve. I had counselling. I'd never had it before, but it was really beneficial. The counsellor helped me to go into the feeling of loss and to experience it. I went to her for about four months. It was good just to talk. In Dublin, I had my close friends to talk to. They would help me, but I don't have friends who would give me that kind of support here in Kerry.

'I do sometimes miss my life in Dublin. As beautiful as Kerry is, it is not my home. I am always going to be a blow-in here. I go to Dublin about four times a year. I need to, because I miss the culture. When I'm there, I'll go to shops and museums, and I'll talk to my friends. I feel so comfortable with them because I've known them for so long.

'I am trying now to make more of a connection with people in Kerry. My life here, so far, has been full of other things. Recently, I set up a network of complementary practitioners with a friend. We contacted people who do counselling, massage, Reiki and reflexology. We meet once a month and just talk.'

Geraldine didn't notice a lot of stigma when she was going through her worst anxiety and panic attacks. 'My friends were very supportive, because they knew I had always been a worrier. They'd seen me panic before exams. Shirley, in particular, was good at making me relaxed. She was very much into having fun and that rubbed off on me. What they did find hard was my spirituality. For a while I stopped going to the pub, and they found my new lifestyle strange. It took them a while to get used to that,

> ❝ If someone had told me back in my days as a career woman, that I'd be living this alternative life, I don't think I would have believed them ❞

and I can understand why. Now, when I'm with my friends, I'll go to the pub and not drink. They're used to me now.

'I do still worry. I now realise that I always will; it's in my make-up. I have to accept that. I worry about my family and their well-being. But I have learned over the years to notice when there is anxiety in my body, but never to get consumed by it. I've learned to detach from it. I meditate every morning, and, when I am feeling stressed, I set an alarm clock for every hour. Then I check in on my body. If it's getting into overdrive, I'll bring it back by breathing or relaxing. It might sound extreme, but I have realised that that is the way I have to live.

'I don't regret my fashion days, but I accept that the life wasn't for me. I learned so much from art college about using my imagination and being creative. I now have a lovely level of creativity in my life, but I'm not feeling under pressure to perform with it. It's a perfect balance. I'm still changing. At the moment I'm concentrating on being more true to myself. That, I now realise, is more important than just being nice.

'I'm glad that I was forced by my anxiety to change my life. I am living an extremely spiritual and a fulfilling life. Were it not for the anxiety, I would have missed out on that. It forced me to look at my life and to what was meaningful to me. I feel grateful to my anxiety for that. I really do. My life is not completely right for me yet, but I'm getting there.'

The things that help
Reiki, meditation and mindfulness
- All these forms of relaxation and healing have become core to my life.

Healthy eating

- Since studying nutrition as part of the course in alternative therapies, I have been very careful with my diet. I'm vegetarian and aware of the food that is bad for me. When you meditate, I think your body becomes more sensitive to toxins. I don't drink regularly, but the odd time I have a glass of wine, I die the next day.

Dancing

- I adore dancing. I'm big into African dance. At the moment I'm doing a course, 'Dancing through the Chakras'. I just love it.

Walking, swimming and surfing

- When I'm out in the country, I feel I am me. I love hill-walking, as well as swimming and surfing. Before I moved to Kerry, though, I took no exercise. Walking to me would have been shopping around town. I am fitter now than I was in my twenties.

Writing my morning pages

- I do my morning pages every day. I find it a great way of focusing my thoughts.

The things that didn't help

Medication (Geraldine refused to take antidepressants)

- At times it was really tempting to give in and to take antidepressants, because life was unbearable. I just didn't want to put anything chemical in my body. I was worried I'd become reliant or addicted to them.

Allergy testing

■ I saw a sign for allergy testing when my anxiety was at its worst in Dublin. I was given a list of the things that I wasn't supposed to eat. When you are feeling down, anxious and a bit confused, limiting your food can be unhelpful. It upset me emotionally. I had to give up a lot of things that were comforting to me. Trying to do that nearly threw me into a larger crisis.

Geraldine's Advice

1. Exercise out in nature.

2. Learn meditation. Become aware of anxious thoughts; recognise that they don't control you, and detach from them.

3. Get to know yourself. Live a life that is in alignment with your values and engage fully with this authentic life.

4. Set up a support system; this can include friends, meditation groups and alternative therapists.

5. Support yourself with people who encourage you with positivity, support and love.

FOR MORE INFORMATION:
Reiki – www.reiki.ie

Mindfulness – www.breathworksmindfulness.org.uk; www.mindfulness-ireland.org

The Artist's Way: A Course in Discovering and Recovering Your Creative Self by Julia Cameron, Pan Books, 1994

CHAPTER TEN
Brian

Brian is a successful businessman of fifty-nine who runs a company with his brother. He is confident and articulate. Yet for the first fifty years of his life, Brian suffered from acute anxiety.

In 1999, Brian had a nervous breakdown. He'd recently moved to a new job as an engineer in a small but aggressive company at the time. He became so anxious, so wary of confrontation, that he felt he could not cope with life any more.

'My job in the company was to look after one particularly difficult and demanding customer. Dealing with him gave me severe symptoms of stress. I had headaches, palpitations and terrible stomach cramps. I was in a meeting one day and I got a message to say that this guy was in reception waiting for me. As I stood up to go to him, I had such a bad pain in my stomach that I almost passed out. I don't know how I got through that day.

'I went to my GP the following day. I said, "I can't go on. I just can't cope with this any more." Everything had become too much. He suggested that I go into St Patrick's Psychiatric Hospital. I wasn't frightened about going in. The anxiety had been going on for so long that I felt maybe this is the time to fix it. Maybe, now, at last I will be cured. It was so nice in there. The bad guys were outside and I did not have to deal with them any more. Meals were provided and there was stuff to do. I had no responsibilities. I was safe.'

❦ The consultant said to me, "You are fifty. People your age don't change very much." He said, "I don't think things are going to get much better." ❦

The in-patient programme, though, was more suited for recovering alcoholics than for nervous patients back then. So although the rest helped, Brian was worried that the cause of his symptoms was not being addressed. 'I went to various therapies within the hospital, but nothing really helped. Back then there was this notion that you cannot get over mental illness. There was no sense that there should be a recovery plan for patients.

'I had always been nervous. I was uncommunicative in a family famed for being sociable. My brother and sister, who were two and four years younger than me, were much more outgoing. My mother worked as a pharmacist, and I didn't get on well with the lady who looked after us, or her with me. I was bullied a bit at school. People picked on you, but it wasn't treated as an issue. I remember one guy really getting my goat. We had this thing that you could challenge someone to a boxing match, and that's what I did. He beat the shit out of me, but it was worth it. At least I had done something about it. And he didn't annoy me as much after that.

'I went on to Blackrock College. I was physically huge; I was over six foot at thirteen, and I loved that. I liked being tall. But I wasn't into sport at all. I hated rugby, and there wasn't much emphasis on anything else. I remember at one time those of us who were not into sport were forced to play soccer for a season. There were very few like-minded people there. Just my best friend and me that I can think of! I did well at school academically. I didn't like learning by rote, but I had an enquiring mind. I was good at science. That is where I shone.

'I was still uncommunicative. I felt socially inhibited and I could not relate to adults. If I was walking up the road and I saw a neighbour, I would cross to the other side. I wouldn't know how to have a conversation. At the back of my mind was this strange fear. I worried that they would find out something about me. I don't know what, but I was terrified I would be found out to be a fool. I was very inhibited with girls. I did go out with a couple of them, but I never kissed them. I always worried, what will they think? I was aware that I was strange, that I couldn't do the things that other people could do.

'My parents were concerned about me; so much so that when I was sixteen they sent me to a psychiatrist. I accepted that they were trying to help me. Medical procedures always seemed natural to me. My mother worked in a hospital and was on first-name terms with the doctors. If anything was wrong with any of us, she would ask them to see us. It was like car maintenance. I went to the psychiatrist for about six sessions, but I never opened up so it didn't help.

'After school, I went to college and things were better. I went to the College of Technology, Kevin Street, and did a London degree in physics and maths. Most of that time was happy. I was living at home in Dalkey, but it was a carefree time. I can't remember being nervous, certainly that was not a problem. That summer when I was eighteen, I went abroad with a friend and I kissed a girl for the first time.

'After I finished my degree, I decided to do statistics as a night course in Trinity College. While I was doing that, I took some part-time jobs in teaching. Some of them were pretty awful. One, in Bull Alley, I couldn't hack at all, so I gave it up after two weeks. Another class, in Ringsend, wasn't too bad and another, for adults, was a dream. It was for adults wanting to take maths. They were really interested in learning and the three-hour class time seemed to fly. After that, I took a teaching job in Dundalk. It was the early seventies and teaching seemed the only option for graduates. But after a year I realised I hated it. The actual teaching was fine for one year; it was interesting implementing my own ideas, but I couldn't bear the idea of doing the same thing for thirty years.

'It became obvious too that I could not handle confrontation. I would get extreme nervous symptoms. I'd have tension in my muscles, palpitations and sometimes stomach cramps, and I'd usually back away from the situation when the symptoms started to kick in. I'd be trying to get the kids to shut up in class. I would hold back initially because there is this whole thing of: this is not going to go well anyway. But my frustration would build up, and every so often I would roar at the kids. My reaction would be all

124

out of proportion, and would not make me feel any better. It made me think that I was not suitable for the teaching profession, so at the end of the school year I decided to leave.

'I was lucky. A local electronics company was recruiting at the time, and I got a job there straight away. I spent a couple of years with them, then moved on, and I coped with

> ❝ Back in my teens I was convinced that I had an ulcer. My mother immediately organised for me to have a barium meal test done, and that showed that I hadn't got one ❞

it all fine. I was dealing with technical issues, and I was good at that. Life was fine on a personal level too. I got married in 1973, having known my wife for just eight months. Our daughter was born in 1978. I stayed in my second technical job until 1982, then I was headhunted to another company. That was great until 1984 when the company went out of business and I was made redundant. There weren't any jobs in Ireland, so we moved to Scotland for a couple of years, but my wife found it hard to settle there so we came home.

'I got a job in County Wicklow in 1986, and that was when all the problems started for me. I went in as an engineer, and for the first time I was supervising people closely. I found that really difficult because of my fear of confrontation. Most of the time I would be inhibited from saying anything, but if a job was not done properly, I would get madder and madder. Then I would explode, and it would not be rational at all. I went to my GP a couple of times during those years. He would put me on sick leave for a week, and say, "We will put down 'exhaustion'." The stigma of nervous illness is so strong. He might prescribe tranquillisers as well. They helped with the symptoms.

'During all that time I was avoiding as many social situations as I could, because parties always brought on my symptoms. I would feel awkward and wouldn't know what to talk about. I tended to socialise more with the people I worked with because we could talk about technical stuff. With them, I didn't have to make small talk.

'Complaining about something on the phone, back then, was a really big deal for me. I'd put it off, and when I did it, I would probably overreact and be rude and uncivilised about it. I would be determined to convince the other person that I was in the right, and they were in the wrong. To do that, I would do everything to try and wound the other person. I didn't see that there are no rights and wrongs – just differences of opinion.

'Then the company I worked for switched the emphasis of their business dealings. Along with a lot of other employees, I was made redundant. That's when I moved to the company in Kildare, and when my symptoms started to take over my life. I did realise that my symptoms were nervous ones; I never thought that the palpitations meant I was having a heart attack. For all that, though, the symptoms are very real. And they can be crippling.

❝ Nervous people get symptoms that are so extreme that they are incapable of functioning in certain situations. They are not imagining their symptoms. They may not have a physical cause, but they are very real ❞

'After my breakdown, I was in St Patrick's for three weeks. My wife visited every day, but it must have been upsetting for her and for my daughter. I felt very safe there, but I was worried that if I stayed there any longer, I might become institutionalised. There were a couple of old-timers there; people who had been in and out several times, and they said, "The doctors won't tell you to go home. You have to ask them yourself if you want to go." That was useful to know.

'Much as I wanted to go home, though, the thought worried

me terribly. I was aware that there wouldn't be any out-patient support. I asked the consultant if I should go for psychoanalysis. He agreed to make an appointment for me to see someone in Blackrock. He said, "I'm not sure if it will do you any good, but you will learn a lot about yourself."

'In the end, though, I never did get to see the psychoanalyst. Because meanwhile I'd started to attend meetings at an organisation called Recovery International. I'd seen a notice up about them in the hospital, and I decided to try going to the meetings in my area. I was so bloody desperate for support, I'd have tried anything. If I'd walked in and they'd asked me to stand on my head in the corner, I would have done it.' (Recovery International was started in America in 1937, at a time when the stigma about mental illness was huge. It tackles the symptoms of nervous illness without worrying about the cause.) 'It was a protective environment, and that helped me. That and the fact that nobody asked for my history. We were only asked for our first names, and everyone was in the same situation. People gave examples of how they had applied Recovery methods in the previous week. They would still get nervous symptoms, but once they understood the system, they would deal with them straight away.

❝ One of the first things you are told is that feelings are not fact, and that symptoms are distressing but not dangerous. When people avoid situations, they are not really afraid of the place or the people; they are afraid of the symptoms. Recovery teaches that the only thing we have to be afraid of in nervous fear is a bit of physical discomfort ❞

'There is a lot of emphasis on routine and following a format. The language sounded strange at first. Nervous people tend to use emotional language and it makes them worse, so the language of Recovery is objective, unemotional and very different. We weren't allowed to use words like "terrible" or "dreadful", and you can't say "this is always happening to me," because that is not strictly true. I found the theory of it all convincing. It's easy to reject a doctor's advice. You tend to think, this guy doesn't know what he's talking about; he hasn't been through it. It is much harder to resist the message of a Recovery meeting, because all these people have been through it.

'Something that was said struck an immediate chord with me. It was "Stop being a complainer." What that meant was that you should not always tell people when you feel bad. All my life I had been told that I should express my feelings; I found that hard, and my tendency to be quiet was almost a criticism levelled at me by my family. Suddenly this guy was implying that my instincts had always been right. I was doing what I should be doing. I felt, this system is for me. There are readings every week, from a book by the founder, Abraham A. Low MD. One week the reading was about the myth of nervous fatigue. Often we might not want to do something because of the fear of failure. If we're reluctant to do it, we persuade ourselves that we just don't have the energy. I had loads of paperwork to do at home, some work-related and some domestic. Every time I went upstairs to do it, I thought, no, I am too tired tonight. I went home after that meeting and got stuck into those papers. I worked for two hours and I was still as fresh as a daisy. And that was when I realised: this stuff works. Within six weeks I was vastly improved and within six months I was a different person altogether.

'Meanwhile I had resigned from my job in Kildare. I'd decided I couldn't ever face going back there. I'd thought I would find another job easily, but it took six months to find work. Life during that time was difficult. Recovery International was the only thing that got me through it. I didn't go into a full-time job, but I started doing some consultancy work. I got a contract for three or four months. I started doing a night class for two nights a week, and while I was doing that, I stopped going to Recovery. I thought, I can hack this now. I can do it.'

Brian's confidence, though, was premature. 'I was working in an engineering capacity, and when things went wrong, I would still get worked up about them. I'd become embarrassed about certain things, like asking for my time-sheet to be signed or putting in an invoice. I was frightened that they might question it. I thought, how will I respond when they do? That fear and insecurity persuaded me that I should go back again to Recovery. I decided that no matter what, I would keep an evening for that free. And things did go smoothly after that.

'In March 2000 I started to do some work for my brother as a consultant. That went smoothly, and after a while he asked me to go into business with him. I said, "Yeah, let's do it." I felt that that was what I should have been doing anyway. We've been in business together ever since. I don't think being supervised would phase me any more. That fear has gone. But having our own business really suits me. When you are the consultant, the expert, people listen to you.

'When you are self-employed, you don't have the luxury of being embarrassed to talk about money. You have got to ring the guy and say, "I will be over later to collect the cheque." Today that doesn't take a feather out of me. I still have my occasional nervous moments; if I do something stupid, I'll be afraid that people will notice. Or when I get a phone call from a customer, the old fear might be there. I think, perhaps something has gone wrong, but then Recovery kicks in. I remind myself that I get lots of calls from this customer, and only a few have been problematic. I realise that it is just my anxiety playing up and the symptoms stop before they take hold.

'In Recovery International we are encouraged to "spot" our behaviour before we get into negative thinking. Often it's the trivialities that nervous people find so hard to manage. I ran out of petrol in the city recently. I had a moment of panic, of thinking what am I going to do? And then I dealt with it in a rational way. I rang the rescue service and they came to get me. Before, I would have thought, how can I get out of this without looking a fool? I'd think, it will all be so embarrassing.'

Brian was so grateful to Recovery International for having changed his life that he was keen to put something back into the organisation. He has been a group leader in County Dublin for almost ten years now and has been the area leader for two years. He is happy to talk about his experiences, but he's not keen to give his full name. 'I don't want my customers to know I once attended St Patrick's Hospital. There is still a stigma around mental illness.'

The things that helped

Attending Recovery International meetings
- Regular attendance was the one thing that really made a difference to me. Without it, I don't know what I would have done.

Tranquillisers
- These helped when my symptoms were particularly bad. Time off work relieved the pressure for me too.

Finding suitable work
- Working as a consultant engineer really suits me. Finding a good working environment helped a great deal.

Having a sense of humour
- You have to learn to laugh at yourself, because some of the reactions you have as a nervous person are really quite ludicrous.

Assertiveness training course
- I tried this before I had my breakdown, so the timing was bad. My symptoms were so strong back then that I couldn't apply the techniques at all. Now I can use some of the methods, and I do find them helpful.

The things that didn't help

Transcendental meditation
- A colleague swore by this, and it had helped my brother when his wife was going through cancer treatment. But it didn't help me at all.

Brian's Advice
1. Treat your mental health seriously. Treat it as a business, not a game.

2. If you can't change an event, change your attitude towards it.

3. Symptoms of panic are distressing. Remember, though, that they are not dangerous.

FOR MORE INFORMATION:
www.recovery-inc-ireland.ie

CHAPTER ELEVEN
Pauline

Born and reared in Dublin, Pauline,* aged seventy-one, lives in rural County Meath. Last year, Christy, her husband of fifty-two years, died. Devastated, she grieved quietly, just as she had when her seventh child died in infancy.

*name has been changed

'I had thought about going to counselling after Christy died,' says Pauline, as we sit at her kitchen table on a sunny autumnal day. 'But then I thought, no I won't. What is counselling? I believe you go in and talk to somebody in the same way I am talking to you now. But what does that do? How does that help?

'Christy died in January 2008. It was the very start of the new year, just after Christmas. He had bad health; he'd taken a heart attack in his sixties. He was a good age. He was eighty-four, fourteen years older than me, but I never expected him to die. It didn't seem like his time. He was due to go to the surgery that morning, just for a routine heart check. He was always up early on surgery days. I was surprised when I woke at 8.30 a.m. I thought, he's not up. I thought, God, something is not right. I leaned over to look at him. Then I came down and did the usual things. I filled the kettle, put on the central heating and put the blinds up. I remember thinking, sweet Jesus, what is wrong? I went back in to the bedroom and I knew that he wasn't right.

'All hell was let loose then. I ran next door for my son-in-law, Peter. He came and he couldn't get a pulse. We rang the surgery, but it was still on the Doc on Call thing. They were there but had forgotten to change the message. After that, I rang a friend who was a nurse. She arrived and went in to Christy. She said, "Yes, he is gone." I'd guessed he was, but I'd needed to have it confirmed. She got in touch with the doctor and everything started up then. All my girls came up. My children all live close by. They were just going back to work after Christmas. My daughters were out there in the driveway crying their eyes out. It was the biggest shock. There was no speaking between us. No talk. Just lots of people coming in and out.

'Everyone was good to me. Friends and neighbours, they were all supportive. A lot of people said to me, "Wasn't it a lovely way to go?" and of course it was. It is what Christy would have wanted: dying in his own bed. But it didn't make up for the fact that he was gone. And it didn't help me at all. I felt I was in the middle of a rough sea; that my life was over. He'd been here all the time with me, someone to talk to and discuss things with. We'd be chatting away, eating our dinner and often people would come in and say, "Oh, you look so cosy!" Those first few months without him were terrible. I'd go shopping and buy too much food. It would end up in the bin. I'd set the table for the two of us. Now I don't sit at the table. I can't bear to see his empty chair. I eat with a tray on my knee.

'I was brought up in Dublin. When my parents wanted to go away alone, they'd dump us with my aunt in Summerhill. I hated it back then – hated it. I hated the very sight of Summerhill. I thought my mother would never come and collect us. When I was older and my cousins came back from Canada, America, or London, they'd come to my mother in Dublin and would not go home unless I went with them. One evening my cousin and her husband were going to a dance in the parish hall. I said "Can I come?" I was fifteen. She said, "Of course," and she gave me a costume, nylons and make-up, and off we went to the dance. You couldn't keep me out of Summerhill after that.

'A year later, my aunt asked my mother if I could go and live with her. She was lonely, with all her family away. My mum wasn't really happy about it because I was an only daughter, but I was thrilled. I hated school and thought my time there would never end, so I jumped at it. I met Christy when I was sixteen. He was a farmer, working for one of the big landowners, as most men around here did at that time. I can't say it was love at first sight. I hadn't experience of what love was, but I liked him very much. He was a fine man. We married when I was seventeen. He worked for Roadstone then and went on working for them until he retired.

'I had my first baby when I was nineteen and a half years old. I had him in Dublin, because it was so isolated where we were living. After that I had a baby every year. I went in to have my third baby on my twenty-first birthday; the labour went over midnight and that was Christy's birthday. I came home, and my mother gave me a late twenty-first birthday party. I had a cake with candles. My three children were there; two at the table and the baby in a Moses basket. I was twenty-seven when I had my eighth child. I didn't want so many, but there was no contraception then. That was it.

'The rural life was very, very hard, but we were happy. It was twice as hard for me coming from Dublin, where there was running water and flush toilets. It was a big shock. To have a bath, we'd have to heat the water in a big skillet pot hung over the open fire – two of those would do it. My parents were good to me. My mother was down with me for a few days, and I was using the bathtub to wash the clothes, scrubbing them on the washboard. I'd be soaked right through. She said, "When I go back now, I will see about a washing machine." There was no phone, so she wrote a note to ask Christy to borrow a van and go up, and I wrote one back. And she wheeled out this twin-tub. It was great, even though we had to fill it with rain water we caught in barrels off the house.

'I made sure my kids were never hungry anyway, and we managed somehow. I had to get them out in the morning and they had to walk two and a half miles to school. I would do the weekly shop on a bicycle on a Saturday, when Christy handed me his pay. I'd have a bag on each of the handlebars and a box at the back, and I would cycle the six miles there and back with all the food for the week. Maybe I would be six or seven months' pregnant. There'd be threepence left over for church the next day. But I was a good manager, thank God, and we never went into debt the way they do now. There'd be the famous parcels from America, where I had cousins. They'd send beautiful clothes for the children.

'I had my sixth child at home. That went well, so I had my seventh at home too. It was a hard birth. He was ten pounds, but everything went well. The birthing nurse was there and the midwife. When they came down the next day to wash the baby, they said he hadn't wet his nappy. They said that was unusual. He was beginning to get jaundice and he wouldn't take a bottle. This was going on for a while, and I began to get worried. I remember heading out when my mother-in-law was nursing the baby. I went up the road to some people who had a phone. It was a long walk, and they weren't at home. I ended up walking the three miles to the surgery in Trim. I thought the doctor would come right away, but he said to just give the baby water, and he'd be there the next day.

'He came the next morning and said that the baby had gastroenteritis. He sent him to a local hospital. I depended on lifts to get up and down, and I got a lift. But when I got to the hospital, the baby wasn't there. He'd been sent to Our Lady's Hospital in Crumlin. A couple of days later, I got a telegram telling me to ring the hospital. My neighbour went up to the house where there was a phone. She rang and they said the baby had died. They needed my permission for a post-mortem, and I said "Of course."

❛ Often though, since, when I heard of those body parts left in a jar, I've thought, Would any of those have been my child? It would have been around the same time, but I didn't follow it up. What would have been the point? ❜

'They discovered it was something to do with his kidneys and was very rare. They told my father later that the post-mortem had really helped them; that they had another baby with a similar condition and they now knew what to do.

'It was very sad. I didn't even get to see my baby. The priest who'd christened him went out to bury him. Christy, my mother and father and some of the neighbours were there. Nobody offered to mind the children so that I could go. I remember them saying, "Maybe you are better off not to go," but I regret that to this day. I've been told he was a beautiful sight. The next day my neighbour and I went on our bicycles to the grave. She brought a lovely bunch of flowers, then she went away and left me there. Seeing the grave tore my heart out. The worst thing, though, was about three weeks later when this pack arrived with all his little clothes from the hospital.

'I went to see the priest who'd baptised him, and he said that I wasn't to grieve. That the baby was now an angel and would be looking after me. People didn't seem to understand that I'd been carrying that baby for nine months. They were more or less saying, "You have enough to rear." I did grieve. Of course I did. I still pray for that baby every night, especially since Christy died. But I had six others depending on me. From morning until night you were just washing and ironing. I often stood in the kitchen late at night ironing all the children's clothes and polishing their shoes to send them to church on Sundays. I used to bicycle to early mass, and Christy would walk with the children the two miles there and back.

❝ I used to be afraid to tell my mother that I was pregnant again. She'd say, "Does that man ever do anything else?" ❞

'My faith is strong now. It's a comfort, but it wasn't back then. I was angry that I'd had so many children. I'd say to the priest, "There should be something for the likes of me." After the eighth child, I said to my doctor, "I can't go on like this." She said, "Oh absolutely," and she fixed me up with something. It was very hush-hush back at that time. But I never felt guilty. I always felt I had done my duty.

'As the children grew, the house was always full. There'd be people in and out, girls and fellows. I'd come home from seeing my mother on a Sunday, and I wouldn't know where to look. They'd all wait for me to come back and give them tea. I remember I felt run-down, and I went to the doctor. He said, "You have how many at home? What are they all doing there?" They were in their twenties. I didn't half-lecture to them about that, but they didn't move out until they got married.

'I was working on and off as a care assistant. I looked after a lady with motor neurone disease who was very sick. But I had no confidence in those days. I'd never go shopping alone. I used to get a lift from a friend. I dreaded going into Dunnes Stores. I'd feel the place going around and be looking for the way out. I never went alone, but if the friend I was with wandered away, I would need to see where she was. My tummy would churn. I'd feel dizzy. I didn't know why that was.

'Christy took a heart attack in his sixties. It frightened him. He wasn't good at coping with pain. When he got a chance for early retirement, he took it. After the last child moved out, I said to Christy, "I'm not feeling secure with all the family gone." I said, "Why don't we move into the village?" But he didn't want to because the house was built on his home place; it was his mother's land. My youngest daughter and her husband were looking for a house in the country at the time. So they moved into our house and built us an apartment on the side. It was the best thing we ever did. We were very happy and content here. We have our own entrance, but we know that they are there.

'I suffered for some years from Seasonal Affective Disorder, SAD. I would dread winter. I wouldn't want to go anywhere; I just could not be bothered. I'd be grouchy and bad-tempered. As for Christmas, if anyone even mentioned it to me, I'd want to scream. I put up with it for a year or two. I did tell my doctor how I was feeling. He said, "That sounds like SAD," but he didn't do anything about it. He suggested I get some special lights, but I couldn't be bothered with all that. I mentioned it again when I was at the surgery for something else. He gave me a tablet to balance things out. That made all the difference. The kids couldn't believe how much better I was. I'd had no interest in anything. They were fed up listening to me, and with the tablet I'd be bright and breezy and calm. I'd take it all winter, then come off it in the summer months.

'I still hate Christmas with a vengeance. I loved it when I was young, and when my children were small, I loved getting all their little presents ready. But as they went away – don't mention it. The minute I see Christmas starting on TV, I turn my head away. I'd get pulled into it, doing the shopping and the present-buying, and I could never get my head around it. I fought against it, but I still had to go through with it. I remember one year I was in such bad form and my son was coming for dinner. You can only get so many around my kitchen table, and I ended up eating by the sink. I was fuming. I'd say "Never again." I'd say that every year. Since Christy died, I have a great excuse. I don't send Christmas cards and I don't bother with a tree or with decorations. Last year I went to a daughter who wasn't doing Christmas either. She was upset because it was almost Christy's anniversary. This year I'm not going to anyone's house. I'm staying in my own place. I will cook something other than turkey, and I'll pretend it's a normal day.'

After the first bad months after Christy's death, Pauline started to get her life together again. 'I started going back to the Third Age Centre. I'm good friends with the woman who runs it. We do all sorts of things there, like "Go for Life," which is keep fit, and Christy and I were volunteers for the Senior Help Line. My friend kept on at me to go down there after Christy died, but at first I didn't want to. Not at first. There are photos of Christy everywhere there. We'd been involved in the drama group and had appeared at the Peacock Theatre. We did samba dancing too and appeared on *Live at Three*. It's nice down there. Eventually I went back. A bus comes to collect me. It's been my lifeline. Often my friend asks me to go with her around the country. We talk about the club in other areas, where there are groups thinking of starting one of their own.

'It's wonderful having my daughter and her family next door. My daughter picks up shopping for me, and she does my hair whenever there's an occasion on. She used to be a hairdresser. She has a daughter of nineteen and a son of seven. That little boy is just a joy to me. He calls me his Supernan. He comes round with his football and says, "Hello, Nanny, how is your leg today? Is it sore? No? Then will you play football with me?" I end up in goal. The other day we were taking a break from football, and I sat up on the trampoline. I couldn't get off and he had to get his mammy. I thought she'd have a fit! I have nine grandchildren, and the kids keep me involved with them all. And that's just brilliant.

'I have a great life now. When I talk to myself, which I tend to do, I think, God gave me these years because I married so young. I didn't have a life of freedom. I miss Christy terribly. I say, "Goodnight" and "Good morning" to him every day. I feel he is around somewhere, and I don't feel I am doing anything wrong when I go out and about. This is my time. I go down to the Centre most days, and I'm back on the Senior Helpline. I've been on holidays with the Third Age Club. This year I've been to Salthill and last weekend we were in Cork. In the spring I went to Spain to visit friends. It's the first time I've been there. I was a bit nervous about going, but it was beautiful and the heat was gorgeous. I may return next year. Our friends had been asking us for years, but towards the end, Christy didn't want to go anywhere.

'We used to go on holidays together with the club, but that all stopped. Christy would wait until the morning we were due to go, then he'd say that he wasn't well enough. Eventually I said to my friend, "We're not going any more." I was sick of the coaxing I'd have to do to get him to go. Instead we'd holiday at home. The family put up decking for us, and I'd take our cooked breakfast and lunch out there. We'd sit in the sunshine, listening to the radio, and it was like being away. It was lovely. We were happy. I'd made up my mind and that was it. And the summer was always good to us. If the weather was fine, Christy would be out pottering in the garden. The winters were harder. He'd just sit in the kitchen. There were times, I have to be honest, when I would say, "When is my time?" Because all the caring seemed to go on and on.

'I do have one big regret. On the day before Christy died, we had a little row. He got cranky those last few days. He wasn't feeling well and he went to bed. I was sitting in here and I heard him calling. Apparently he had been calling for some time, but I hadn't heard him. He was angry with me, and I said, "Christy, I am doing my best. Don't shout at me." And afterwards, I went into silent mode. He got up later, but I didn't speak. I was fed up. I didn't answer when he said he was going to bed. And when I went up later, his eyes were following me around the room. They were sorrowful, as if he was saying "Sorry" to me. It never occurred to me to say, "Do you want a drink?" He didn't say he wanted anything, but I think about that now. I got into my own bed. There was just a dresser between us, and if he made a move at all, I'm sure I'd have heard him. I was very alert. He depended on me quite a lot. He kept watching me, then he sighed and turned towards the wall. I remember his eyes.

'I have and I haven't come to terms with that. I wish I could turn back the clock, but I can't do that. I have to live with it. Every night I say "Sorry" to Christy. Whether he hears me or not, I don't know, but it gets it out of myself. It does bother me a lot. We had so many years together. We had a huge celebration for our fiftieth wedding anniversary. We had lots of good times, and there were times when there was stress with the family. Sometimes I get a bit overcome. I look over at his chair, and say to myself, "Where are you?" But I have a certain prayer I say, and I ask God to let Christy watch over me. And I feel he is. I feel very much that he is close by.

'When we got married, janey mack, we had two tea chests nailed on top of each other. We had one plate each. Now the kids are moaning about this, that and the other. If they marry, they won't go into a house unless it has absolutely everything. When I would have problems, or felt down, the only contact I had with my mother was through a letter. She would never know. I often say that to my family, because their problems immediately land on my back. They'll ring, and we'll have a normal conversation. Then I'll say, "Anything strange?" That is giving them the opener to say whatever is troubling them. They unload on me and worry me as well. But that, I suppose, is what being a mother is about.

> ❝ When I feel down, I have an idea that this is a black hole to go through. I'll go through it, and face it, and know there will be light at the end of the tunnel ❞

'The weekends are the only time I feel really lonely. If there's racing on the TV, I switch over. That was something Christy would really enjoy. Down moments do happen. Sometimes I will be reading at night and my thoughts will trail. And I will be going over the day when Christy died, and the "what if"s and all this. I said to the doctor, "Could he have been calling me? Could he have suffered? Because I'm usually alert when he moves." He said, "No, he was very peaceful. He was lying with his hand under his chin." He said it was like someone switching off a light, and he wouldn't have known anything. I try to hang on to that thought. It has given me some comfort.'

The things that helped

Tablets for SAD

■ They're very mild, and it's a small dose. I don't want to tell you what they are, but I won't think of going off them now. Why should I when they make me feel so much better? They are wonderful and are letting me live.

Volunteering for the Senior Helpline

■ I get great pleasure from that. We don't give advice, but when the caller has finished talking to you, you feel that they've enjoyed it. You feel that it's eased the pressure of whatever was bothering them and maybe given them some turnaround. Maybe you share something that happened to you and that gives them an option. In the training, we're taught not to take the problems home with us. We'll discuss the calls with our colleagues, then leave the stress behind.

The Third Age Club (formerly Active Retirement)

■ The club has given me so much confidence. Last weekend I had to travel from Cork to Dublin alone and then go home on the bus. I would never have been able to do that during my marriage. I'm now happy to shop alone too.

Reading

■ I've always loved reading. When I was a child I read comics, and when I was first married I read the classics in my aunt's house. I'd take one down when Christy went to work and still be reading it when he was due home. I only read at night now. I love books by Catherine Cookson and Josephine Cox. As long as I have a book to read, I'll never need sleeping pills.

Having the family close by

■ I do worry about intruders. You hear such terrible things these days. When I hear my daughter's family come in on a Sunday and I know that they are settled, I can go to bed and read in absolute contentment.

Pauline's Advice

1. When you feel low, remember it won't last. There is light at the end of the tunnel.

2. Get out and about. Keep active, then you won't have time to brood.

3. Volunteer. Helping other people will help you too.

FOR MORE INFORMATION:
The Senior Helpline – www.seniorhelpline.ie (1850 440 444).

Age and opportunity – for details of classes for older people – www.olderinireland.ie

CHAPTER TWELVE
Senan

Senan,* aged sixty, from Ennis in County Clare suffers from bipolar disorder. He copes with his illness thanks to an excellent mental health service provided by the HSE. He finds solace too from AWARE, the support group for people with depression. He says that sharing his experience with others is invaluable.

*name has been changed

When the Ryan Report on institutional child abuse was made public in May 2009, Senan became upset. It brought back painful memories of his time in a national school run by the order of Christian Brothers. 'I'm talking about physical abuse, about corporal punishment,' says Senan. 'I was badly beaten from first class, when I was six. We'd get a thump if our lessons were wrong. I wasn't hit every day, but the biggest part was the fear. If someone else was being hit, you were watching, and you knew you could be picked on next.

'It could be a spelling mistake, or maybe you'd missed a line of poetry. You'd get pulled up, and you might get a slap across the back of the head or across the jaw. I don't remember getting the leather in first class, but certainly we were hit with that too from second class. I remember the pain of the leather across my hand. I remember the pain and the humiliation. The beating made me feel inferior. It gave me bad self-esteem. For six years I never ever asked to leave the classroom. I didn't have the courage to say, "Can I go to the toilet?" I'd sit there all morning, go home at lunchtime and rush for the toilet. I'd do the same in the afternoon.'

Senan was the youngest boy in his class. He arrived at the school in first class, having spent the first six years of his life in County Mayo. 'My father was a County Clare man, but he went to work in County Mayo, and he met and married my mother there. He moved back to County Clare in advance of the rest of the family. I remember him coming to explain what was happening, that we would be following in a while. I was very sad that my father was leaving. I remember when he left he gave me a piece of chalk. He used it in his work shoeing horses. I don't remember being in Mayo without him, but I do recall seeing the removal lorry about three months later.

'I have scant recollection of Mayo. I don't remember much about school. But I do remember making my First Communion there. I had chicken-pox and after the service I had to go home. I remember my mother saying I couldn't go to the party. That just stuck in my head.

'I was happy at home in County Clare. It was good being there with my two brothers and my sister. It was the abuse at school that was the problem. I remember one priest in particular. This was later on, when I was in fifth class. He'd remove you and take you up to his desk. He'd sit you beside him, and he'd correct your exercise. When he came to a mistake, he'd slide his hand up your thigh along your short pants; we used to wear short pants then until we were thirteen. He never touched my private parts, but he'd get very close to it. Then he'd give you a hard pinch.

'We all felt terrorised at that school. It wasn't just the beatings. There were the derogatory remarks too. Those came all the time to everybody. I didn't learn at that school. I couldn't. I was too frightened. We were never carefree. Two or three of us would stand at the side of the playground and talk about comics, but we were always subdued. We wouldn't run around smiling and happy. The environment wasn't conducive to that. We knew what we'd be facing when we got back inside.

'I told my parents about the beatings. I think most boys in the country did. But we were told that we deserved it. "Father whatever, if he hit you, he must have had a reason." My father trusted all the teachers; in this country they were God. And we felt helpless. It wasn't just the priests. The lay-teachers were no angels either. There was only one teacher who didn't blackguard us. I met him recently in Ennis. I thanked him for being good to us. I said, "You were a gentleman, a gentleman amongst a very bad bunch and I've never forgotten it." He said, "Oh, Senan, that was a terrible era."

❝ I've kept up contact with five others who went through the system with me. I've bumped into them all since the Ryan Report came out; we've discussed it and replayed our experiences. One lad says he feels the only way he'll get it out of his system is to burn the building down ❞

'My mother suffered from rheumatoid arthritis. She was in hospital a lot when I was a child, in a home that had been a geriatric hospital. She'd be there for maybe two or three months at a time. We'd have her home with us for six months, then maybe she'd have to go back in again. That was hard. I was always close to my mother. My father used to arrange dinner in the middle of the day. He'd come home from work, and we'd all go into a café. Then he had only to do something light for us in the evening. We all helped him to clean, to tidy and to hoover.

'I went on to secondary school when I was twelve. I did two years there. It was run by the Christian Brothers, but that school was like Butlin's compared to the one we had left. They used the leather there, but there was no punching. It seemed too late, though, to learn. I'd been too frightened for too long to become interested. After the two years I came out of the secondary-school system, and I went to a vocational school. That was more hands-on. I learned mechanical drawing, woodwork and metalwork. We did agricultural science too. I enjoyed that, absolutely.

'I had happy times as a teenager. I was interested in music. I loved all kinds, but this was the era of the Big Band. I remember when I was sixteen, a big band was coming to town. I was allowed to go. It was my first dance. I remember my mother saying, "Ah, go on! It's not a regular thing." We were all into traditional music. My eldest brother, Paddy, played the trumpet with a show band. I play the accordion. When Paddy came home on holidays from America, we'd clear out the sitting-room. We'd get two or three musicians in, and we'd all dance on the lino. Paddy often says, "How did we all fit in?" The room was only fourteen-foot square.

'In 1966, when I left the vocational school at seventeen, I worked in an aviation company as a trainee in metallurgy. I was taught how to read the different types of metal formation. I learned the difference between a good bolt and a bad one. A year later, in 1967, I went to London and got a job at the Irish Centre in Camden Town. The centre catered for people who were looking for work. We were giving them services as well as putting them into employment. My work was to identify where people might possibly get a job. I contacted the big industries in the area, as well as the hoteliers. I helped a lot of Irish girls who were arriving in London wanting jobs as waitresses or cleaners. It was an interesting and a responsible job. I was good at it. I loved it, but I did wonder what I might have achieved had I better qualifications, had I had a better chance at school.

'I spent five happy years in London. I met and married my wife there. We met at an Irish dance. We were both twenty-two. It was pretty much love at first sight. She wasn't my first girlfriend, but I'd say she was my first serious one.

'We went back to Ireland then. A multinational company was starting up in County Clare. I applied and they were impressed with the experience I'd gained in England. They liked that I'd had to approach companies, have meetings and refer people on. They offered me a job as a buyer. The company eventually employed three hundred and fifty people. I had to buy machinery, find electricians and employ groundsmen. There were four of us; two were senior to me, although by the time I left I was number two.

'I loved the job. It was great money and with good travel. For the first couple of years I travelled around Ireland, but after that I went to France, Germany and Switzerland. When the man who employed me retired, I sent him a card. I said, "I hope you have a wonderful retirement, because you gave me such a good life when you employed me." I said, "If I had gone out the door that day without a job, I probably wouldn't have earned half the money." He was astounded. He said, "I never looked at it like that."

'My mother died in 1977. She had stomach cancer. My wife and I went to visit, and we could see there was something very wrong. The nurse said we should notify the family. We drove home and rang America to tell my two brothers. I'll always regret that decision. We lived twenty-three miles away from the hospital and, when we got back, my father met us in reception. He said my mother had passed away.

❝ My brothers came home, and one of them never shed a tear. I thought, I came away from my mother's bedside for you and you can't even cry for her. I never said it to him, but I still think about that ❞

'My wife and I were happy together. We'd had two sons soon after we returned to Ireland. Life was good, but I had periods of depression. Occasionally I needed time off; just one or two weeks at a time. I'd be feeling lonesome and not sleeping well. I couldn't relax, and my wife would be worried.

'I'd have constant diarrhoea. I was sent to Dublin to have that investigated. I went to the Jervis Street Hospital. They did tests for three weeks. I remember I had a barium test, and another one where I had to lie on one side, then the other. It was horrible! And nothing showed up. They said, "I think you are a bit highly strung." They said I had to learn to relax. The doctor said, "Take life easier than you do at the moment." He said, "You have two children. I can see the scenario; I can imagine you picking up toys constantly." He said, "Don't be doing that. It's not clutter." He was right, of course! They sent me home with prescriptions for Lomotil to help the diarrhoea and Valium to help me relax. They gave me a year's prescription, but I stopped taking it after five or six months.

'I saw two different psychiatrists over the years. I saw the first privately at his house. He said I should think about changing my job. He said, "There is too much responsibility for you. It's too pressurised." He told me I had the wrong personality for a job like that. I didn't want to hear that. I stopped seeing him after a while. A year or two later when I felt anxious again, I saw a different psychiatrist. He gave me drugs to take for two months and said I would be fine. He said, "I don't need to see you again."

'My sister had died in 1987. That was terrible. I miss her every single day. Then in November 1996 my father died. He was a very special man. Life hadn't been easy for him. It was hard for him when we were small and my mother was in hospital, and he was young when he became a widower. He never married again, but he had a lot of friends. He'd go and mix with them; that's what kept him going.

'Early in 1997 things began to go pear-shaped. I was put on the famous Prozac. I was on it for a month or six weeks, but I felt no different. My doctor sent me to a psychologist. I spoke to her for a month or so, but she was more or less saying what the first psychiatrist had said. She said I should change my work and my lifestyle. I just didn't want to hear that. It wasn't going to happen.

'In May of that year I became very emotional. I was at work and started crying. I felt weak and cold, yet I was sweating profusely. I was so tired. I'd had a bad sleep pattern all year, and I just wanted to go home. My boss said, "Are you okay?" I said, "I don't think so. I have to get home." He said, "I don't think you're in any fit state to drive." He rang the company nurse, and she came over. She said, "Are you taking something?" I asked her what she meant and she said, "Are you taking any medication?" I told her I was on Prozac and she asked me what it was for. I found that unbelievable. She was a friend of mine but that left a sour taste.

'My boss drove me to my GP. She said, "You'll have to go to hospital." She lay me down and explained that she'd ring St John of God's psychiatric hospital in Dublin to see if they had a bed. She said, "Go home. Lie down and get ready to go." This was late in the morning. She rang me later to say they had a bed, and I was to be there by ten that evening. So my son, his wife and my wife drove me to Dublin. That was terrible. Terrible for them, and for me. I was in there for seven long months.

'The doctors treated me with various mixes of drugs. They said I was difficult to treat, that I seemed to be drug-resistant. We had a lot of occupational therapy, and I found that good. I discovered I was a carpenter and I'd never known it. I made all sorts of stuff. I made a wheelbarrow and a planter. I saw the psychiatrist once or twice a week, but I only saw a psychologist once. I couldn't understand that. After the first three months I was allowed home at weekends. My wife used to drive up every Friday and bring me home. I'd spend Saturday at home and on Sunday, first thing, we'd have to head back again.

'My boss came to see me once in hospital and that was it. People did know where I was, my wife had no reason to hide it. If I'd had a bypass, everyone would have been ringing to say, "How is he getting on?" But because it was a mental illness, they would never ask after me. It was the same when I came out. If I met a colleague even five or six months after getting out, they would walk across the street and keep going. A few would say, "Hello. How're you?" But they don't know how to handle mental illness. There's a stigma and a lack of education about it. Nobody said, "How did you get on in hospital?" Nobody, apart from my immediate family.

> **❝ I had no flowers, no get-well cards, no phone calls or messages of sympathy. I might as well have been in Mountjoy Jail ❞**

'I went back to St John of God's to see the psychiatrist after my discharge. I went every month. I made three visits, then he said he wanted me seen more regularly. He said, "You should see someone in County Clare." He referred me to a private psychiatrist. She saw me three or four times in as many weeks. Then she said, "I can't deal with your case without more support. You need to go to Ennis Hospital." She arranged that. I've been under their care ever since, and that care, under the HSE, has been excellent. I'm looked after by a team. I see a consultant psychiatrist, a psychologist, a social worker and an occupational therapist. I see a care nurse manager too and I have group relaxation. I see each of them every two weeks, more if I need it. I could not fault them.

'It was decided when I was in St John of God's that I should not go back to my job. At the time, that was devastating. And the company didn't get in touch to suggest a compromise. I had six months with full pay, then six months on half-pay. Then that was it. After that one visit from my boss, there was no contact from work. I feel bitter about that. The company employed a full-time taxi. It was a private operator, but he was on call and could drive anyone anywhere. That car was never once put at my wife's disposal. It would have helped her so much when she needed to visit me. I had a good time at that company, but I was just a number. Eventually I had a phone call to say they were offering me voluntary redundancy because I wasn't returning to work. I think they were afraid that I'd sue the company.

'I now have a clerical job here in Ennis. I work five mornings a week and that suits me fine. My supervisor, Mary, knows that I have depression and she is very good to me. If for some reason I can't go to work in the mornings, I work in the afternoons instead. Mary is very understanding – she lost a brother to suicide.

'Four years ago my mood dipped badly. When I'm on an even keel, my medication controls the condition, but when it drops drastically, nothing seems to work. They told me I needed ECT, and they wanted to admit me to the Ennis Acute Psychiatric Hospital. I didn't want to go. The doctor said that if I agreed to go in for ECT on Monday, Wednesday and Friday for two weeks, I could stay at home. I gave my undertaking. It made my memory bad for a while, which was frustrating, but it did lift my mood.'

Senan's next crisis came three years later. 'That time I was so down and depressed that I didn't even know where I was. I didn't recognise anybody. I had ECT in March and April. And I was back in hospital for two weeks in September. When I'm really low, nothing helps. I never have highs, but I've now been diagnosed with bipolar disorder.

'At the moment I see the consultant psychiatrist every two weeks. If I have a problem, though, I can ring and see him in between. I don't make a habit of that, but it's good to know the service is there. I have access to a crisis nurse in the acute psychiatric unit too. I can see her twenty-four hours a day. And I do sometimes avail of her services. I was there on a Friday night last time I went through a bad patch.

'I see the psychologist and the social worker every two weeks. The psychologist asks me how my mood has been and how I have been coping. She asks me if anything in particular has upset me. We spent a lot of time discussing physical and corporal punishment when the Ryan Report came out. I found that extremely helpful. I see the care nurse every two weeks. She asks me how my meeting with the psychologist went, and she checks whether I'm happy with the level of my medication. I see her before the Tuesday meeting of the psychiatric team. If I want a particular issue brought up in that meeting, the care nurse will tell the team.

'It's been a long and difficult road. I'm managing, but I feel the bad bouts of depression are getting worse. When I'm low, I'm in an isolated, dark place. I get suicidal thoughts. That can happen often. I don't talk to my wife about it. I can't mention it to her or to my two sons. When they ask me how I'm feeling, I say, "Not too good today." That is the end of it. It's easier to talk to outsiders. I took a lot of tablets one night. Nobody knew about it. I went to bed early on a Friday night and told my wife I would sleep in on Saturday. That is not too unusual for me. She woke me at four the next day, and I realised the tablets hadn't worked. She didn't know what I had tried, and I didn't tell her. I tried it because I was in pain and was looking for peace. I woke that day in better form than I'd been in when I'd gone to bed.

'I'm huge into my family. I have four grandchildren, two boys and two girls. I'm mad about them. Two of my grandchildren are always at home. My wife minds them every second week. I was at the cinema with them yesterday afternoon. We saw a new cartoon. I love to spoil them.

❝ They assured me that whatever way I was feeling, somebody in the group would have felt that same way. Maybe somebody still was ❞

'I've been going to AWARE, the support group for people with depression, since 1998. The canteen manager where I work told me about it. She'd been hospitalised, and when she heard I'd been in too, she explained about the group. She said, "Would you like to try it?" I remember going that first time. They were very welcoming. They showed me that I was in a safe, confidential place. If I wanted to speak, I could; if not, that was okay too. They understood pretty much everything that I had been through, and they were there to help.

'I go to AWARE every week, unless something really important crops up. It means that I can go out and sometimes have light conversations and some- times have not so light-hearted conversations. There may be tears. If you are having a bad day, the other people will know what that feels like. They'll tell you that there will be good days, that you won't always feel the way you are feeling tonight. They'll say, "There will be light at the end of the tunnel." We exchange tips too. But we're careful to say, "Just because it worked for me doesn't mean it will necessarily work for you." We always end the session with tea and coffee. That is important. We chat about all sorts of stuff. That part might go on for an hour.

'I now trust the professionals. They know what they're talking about, they're dealing with mental illness all the time. About two years ago I tried to come off my medication. I was feeling good at the time, and I didn't mention it to the doctors. Afterwards, I carried on feeling good for a while. I lasted for maybe three or four weeks. Then things started to go wrong again. It would take another six weeks to start feeling better again. It just wasn't worth it. I dislike having to take the tablets and find a glass of water. At the same time, it helps. I know that I really do need them.'

The things that helped

Medication
- I'm now on Lithium to control my mood, Rivotril for stress, Zispin and Stilnoct for sleep. Most of the time, that combination works well for me.

Group relaxation
- I have group relaxation every week through the HSE psychiatric team. I find that extremely good.

AWARE
- AWARE is a wonderful support. We meet every week.

When you see a psychiatrist, you know they have probably never felt depressed. They don't know how it feels. Everyone in AWARE understands.

Music

■ Music is better than any tablet. I listen if I want to improve my mood. At the moment I have a selection of James Last on my CD player. I like a lively tune, something easy and beautiful, rather than something emotional. It will always give me a lift. I listen to music when I'm driving, and I'll tap away. There's great power in it.

Exercise

■ It's hard to get the motivation going to take exercise. When I'm not feeling good, it's the very last thing I want to do. In June 2009 I was doing pretty well. My daughter-in-law and myself did a semi-official 10-kilometre walk. That was good, but I haven't managed to do very much since.

Keeping a mood diary

■ This idea came from a previous psychologist. You write down how you feel. You rate your thoughts on a scale of one to a hundred. You make columns and go through the different ones asking yourself, why did I feel like this? Did I feel the same yesterday? What do I need to do now to change my mood? You list the things you know help you to get out of a bad patch.

Reiki

■ Someone in AWARE said they'd found Reiki very good for depression. I tried it and found it great.

Massage

- I used to go to a woman for massage and I'd always fall asleep at the table. The massage took an hour. She'd leave an extra fifteen minutes, then she'd wake me and say, 'Senan, it's time to go.'

Family support

- My family has always been there for me. They understand. And that is terribly important to me.

The things that didn't help

Books

- I've read a few books on depression. I don't really find them helpful. I don't use websites either, except to check out new drugs.

Acupuncture

- Some people in AWARE swear by acupuncture. I tried it, but it didn't work for me.

Drink

- I'm not a habitual drinker. I will have a drink maybe once every six months with a neighbour. And if someone comes to the house, I'll have some wine or maybe a beer. But I'd never drink regularly at home. I'd worry that if I did, it would become habitual.

The things people say

- It's never helpful when people tell you to pull yourself together. You would if you could, but if you have severe depression, you can't.

Senan's Advice

1. Attend a support group.

2. Never stop your medication unless your consultant advises you to.

3. Take regular exercise.

4. Be kind to yourself; remember that you are very special.

FOR MORE INFORMATION:
AWARE – www.aware.ie (01 661 7211)

CHAPTER THIRTEEN
Margaret

Margaret,* aged forty-two, is a special needs teacher from Naas, County Kildare. She has suffered from anxiety disorder for the past sixteen years. Since her worst episode, she has turned to an energy psychologist for help. While she is not 'cured', Margaret's quality of life has greatly improved.

*name has been changed

In September 2008 Margaret knew her workload was going to increase dramatically. She felt so stressed as she prepared for the start of term that a week beforehand she simply couldn't get out of bed. 'I had come off my antidepressant medication at the time,' she says. 'I was pushing and pushing myself to get everything done in time, but it all got too much. I realised then that I had to do something about my anxiety. It was my turning point.'

We meet in a luxury hotel in Naas. Dressed smartly in black, Margaret appears calm and relaxed. She's so self-possessed that it's hard to believe she suffers badly with anxiety. And that, she tells me, can be a problem. 'People don't understand,' she says. 'Even professionals, I've sometimes felt, haven't accepted what I was going through. It's so hard for anyone to empathise, unless they too have been through it. I don't really like talking about it. I find it hard reliving the bad times, but if talking to you helps even one person, it will have been worthwhile.'

The fifth of six children bought up near Dundalk, Margaret describes her early childhood as fairly standard. 'Ours was a strict family. We were pretty regimented, but that was fine,' she says. 'I didn't know anything different. When I was in my teens, though, my father became an alcoholic. When I look back now, I can see that he suffered from anxiety too. There were places he wouldn't go to, and he found social situations quite difficult. He drank to get through it, and at first that was positive. It helped him. But, over time, his drinking became invasive to family life. My four older siblings were moving out at this stage; there was just me and my younger brother left at home. It was a difficult time. Mum would put up with a huge amount. She held the family together. She was great at keeping things ticking over. She'd continue to manage, but she never tried to force my father to stop drinking. She just lived with it. It got to a stage where I didn't want to live at home any more.

'Money became a bigger issue. My father held down a full-time job, but he was going for extended lunches. We'd know he was the worse for wear when he walked in. Everything felt uncomfortable, but nobody was talking about it. We were not a family who got into the nitty-gritty of things. I never had friends round; I felt I couldn't. But it wasn't a social house anyway, because we lived in a rural area. And asking friends home was discouraged. I didn't talk to anyone about my father's drinking. I was too embarrassed. I just got on with life and made the best of it. I was always bubbly and I wanted to be involved in everything. I really looked forward to leaving home and going to college.

'My sister was living in Dublin at the time. When I got a place at UCD (University College Dublin) to study social science, I moved in with her. That was "wow!" It was brilliant. I loved the course and looked forward to being a social worker. I met my first real love at that time. He'd been training to be a priest, but had stopped by the time we'd met. Life was good. I had to go home at weekends, though, because I needed money for the following week. I remember feeling beholden. By this time my father's drinking was chronic. He drank every day for long periods. He'd always covered it up well, but, as time went on, he didn't manage to cover it up as well. But I don't think he realised that.

'It came to a head when my brother, a doctor, finished his medical training. He and my mother discussed the situation and he threatened to have my father sectioned. I'd had enough of it all by then, as well. I was feeling stronger and able to say what I needed to. It was easier now that I had somewhere else to go. And it worked. My father agreed to stop, and he went cold turkey at home. I remember he took to the bed quite a bit, but he'd have done that anyway. If he'd drunk an awful lot one day, he would stay in bed for the next.

'I left college and it was a case of getting a job wherever I could. I moved out of social work for a while and got a management job. Then I met Peter through a friend, and we were inseparable from the time we met. We fell totally in love. It was like we were meant to be together, and it has always felt like that. We married a couple of years later and lived in County Cavan. Peter is eight years older than me. He's steady and reliable and that was part of the attraction. But he's good fun as well. In the twenty years we've known each other, we've only spent two or three days at a time apart. We married a couple of years after we met.

'I got pregnant when I was twenty-six. It was something I wanted, but it was a huge change. I worried about the uncertainty of what I was facing. It seemed an overwhelming responsibility. I worried that I was taking on a being who'd be totally reliant on me. I wanted to be the very best for my child, to be the perfect mother. The anxiety just built up. I found it hard to be alone. I thought, what is going on here?

'I was working as a residential social worker in Cavan at the time. That was difficult, stressful work. I was dealing with teenage girls from all sorts of backgrounds and difficult homes. I'd go into work every day and not know what would happen next. It could be glue-sniffing or arm-cutting. I never knew what I would face. It was a combination of that stress and worry that I'd be a good mother that was making me anxious.

'I didn't like going home alone, and I didn't like being alone there. When Peter is there with me, everything is fine; it always is and always has been. I could cope by myself, but often if Peter had to go out, he'd drop me at my sister's house twenty-five miles away. He was always conscious about what was going on, and he has always been understanding.

'I assumed that once the baby was born, everything would be fine. I thought, I'll be grand. And having baby John did help. I became so engrossed with him that I didn't have time to focus on myself. But John was a difficult baby. He slept very little. Looking back, I wonder if we were feeding off each other's stress. At the time, I was worried that my anxiety during the pregnancy had affected his character. Of course I needn't have. Now, at sixteen, he is the most laid-back kid you could meet.

'Having your first baby, though, changes everything. It's something that isn't talked about a huge amount. I think everyone assumes having a baby will be wonderful, but I was shocked when my life changed completely. Maybe I was selfish before John was born. Certainly, I resented the way everything was turned upside down. That doesn't mean I didn't love him to bits; I did, but it was, oh my God! My body had changed and I didn't know who I was any more. I thought, am I a mother or a wife?

'I didn't go back to work. Peter got a promotion and started working in Dublin, and we moved from Cavan to near Naas in County Kildare. I just coped at home. Peter would go to work each morning. It was a lonely time. I've always been social. I tried to get out and meet people, but the anxiety would always be there. I felt, I don't want to go out. I don't want to go anywhere because I might feel panicky and need to get out quickly. I wasn't prepared to give in to the anxiety, though, so I'd go out, but the panic would be bubbling away underneath. When I say I didn't give in, I mean I'd go to a certain radius from my house and would not go beyond it. I'd keep within my comfort zone. I wouldn't go much beyond Naas. I'd avoid shopping centres, and I'd never go to Dublin without Peter.

> **And there was Peter carrying on his life as normal. It didn't seem fair when I was in this turmoil**

'If I'm in a supermarket and I panic, I feel vulnerable. I get a surge of adrenaline and my hands go all sweaty. I know I need to be calm, but the more I try to be, the more the adrenaline cranks up. I never imagine I'm dying. It's not about that, but I'm terrified of looking silly, of doing something that will make me different from everyone else. I think everyone is aware of how I feel. I think they're all looking at me, or, if they're not, I imagine they would all be looking if they were aware of how I felt. Or if I needed to get out of the supermarket fast, I'd imagine they'd all notice me leaving and know why I'd gone.

'When John was around a year old I went to see my GP. I told him about my anxiety and he suggested that I see a psychiatrist, a private guy who used to come to Naas, but actually I found it a waste of time. I'd say, "I really need help here." I'd tell him that I wasn't coping, but he just talked to me. It was like an ordinary chat, and I felt it was doing me no good. I don't think he understood the impact of my anxiety on my life. I was telling him my problems, but I felt there was no connection between what I was feeling and his understanding of that.

'I was looking for practical things that I could do to manage my condition. I was explaining that I was finding it hard at home to get all the routine things done. I said, "It's hard going." I always remember one of the things he said to me. He said, "Okay, you're driving along, and you feel a panic attack coming. Just

❝ When I panicked, I just wanted to go home. I needed to get to a safe environment, and he just didn't understand where I was coming from ❞

pull in. It's simple." That was the last thing I ever felt able to do. That, I think, is the problem with fear.

'After that, I was given antidepressant medication. I was reluctant to take it. I wouldn't describe my condition as depression, but when you're dealing with constant anxiety, with recurring panic attacks, it gets wearing. Your whole system is fighting, and that is where the antidepressants help. They get you to a stage where you are actually coping, where you are managing with daily life.

'I had my second child, Fiona, three years later. I came off the antidepressants for the pregnancy, and it went well. I was working from home at that time. I'd established a clothes business selling from the home, and I was really enjoying that. I've always enjoyed meeting people, and this way I could do so and stay at home. I love clothes, so it just suited me at the time. It kept me busy and in my comfort zone. Eventually, though, I realised that I wasn't achieving a whole lot. I liked it, but I wanted to have a job where I could get up in the morning and be with other people. I wanted to enjoy that and then to go home.

'After Fiona was born, my GP sent me for Cognitive Behavioural Therapy. That was at St Patrick's Hospital and it was very good. I was set goals to meet every week. It was tough though. If you'd committed to putting strategies in place in a particular week, you had to do it. You didn't go back and say, "I chickened out." I remember going one week and the girl saying to me, "If you're not going to do what I tell you, there's no point in your coming here." It was hard to listen to, but I knew she was right. She did help, she got my anxiety to a certain level and it was definitely beneficial at the time.

'When Fiona started school at four and a half, I started looking for a job. In a local church leaflet, I saw an ad for someone to work with a child with special needs. I liked the idea. I have a nephew with autism, and I've always had a desire to nurture within me. That's why I studied social sciences. My job in the residential home had been too tough. When I had to leave there because we moved, I'd been relieved. I hadn't felt like getting straight back to a job like that. But eight years had passed, and this sounded perfect. I was keen to start helping people again.

'The child was eight. She was a tough little cookie, but I adored working as her classroom assistant. I really loved it. There was a special needs unit attached to the school, and that's where I worked. But as a classroom assistant, I couldn't dictate how the child was taught. I got frustrated, because I felt things could have been handled better. So after a year, I got a job in a specialist school in Naas. That meant a big change in my life. The job as a classroom assistant had been for the mornings only and this job was full-time. But I was fascinated by the whole area of special needs and was eager to learn more.

'I spent a year studying in Trinity College Dublin. I absolutely loved that. Peter was marvellous. He drove me in every Saturday morning and collected me at the end of the day. Without him I would never have managed it. Eventually I left that school in Naas and moved to another one. It was harder work, but I was happier there. I had more control and became totally caught up in it. You get so much back from the children. It's wonderful to see the progress they make, and it stopped me focusing on my own problems.

'My anxiety hadn't gone away. It was still churning away as an undercurrent to my life. But as long as I could cope with my routine, as long as my anxiety didn't make me change the way I lived my life, I'd feel I was coping and managing. I was still on antidepressants. I'd been on them all the time, except when I was pregnant with Fiona. At one stage I went to the doctor because the tablets I was taking affected my libido. He changed them to Effexor, and those really suit me. I have no side-effects with them at all.

'I've tried various things to help my anxiety over the years. I've done courses in meditation. I've tried yoga. And I did a course in aromatherapy. The meditation helped, but it was time-consuming. I dropped it when my life was going well. I didn't get on with yoga, but I loved the aromatherapy. I still use the oils. I find them extremely beneficial.

'I'd always hoped I could manage without medication. And in 2008, I was feeling really well. So at the start of the summer I stopped taking the pills. I really thought that I would be okay. And I was for a while, but then everything started to fall apart. We went on holiday to France, and the anxiety was definitely there. We came home and I started preparing for the school year. I had a new project to work on, and I was worried I wouldn't cope. Peter was a great help to me, both practically and emotionally. But there was a lot to organise, and it became extremely stressful. A lot of people were depending on me and that was a worry. I thought, what happens if I can't cope? What will the other teachers think of me? How will I ever explain?

'When I woke on that Monday morning, I said, "I can't get up. I cannot get out of bed, it's all got too much." I said, "I can't face the thought of school starting next week." That was the first time ever that I'd felt like that. It was a serious place to be. Peter was wonderful. He got the children up and off to school, then he went to work. I stayed in bed for a while, then I got up feeling angry with myself. Why had I given in instead of fighting on as I'd done the week before?

'At the same time though, it was a release. I'd admitted, okay, I can't do this, I don't want to do this. Peter rang his mum. He's close to her, and she was aware I suffered from anxiety. He'd discussed it with her several times before. He contacted my sisters and brothers too. It was important for him to share the problem. It had always been hard for him, carrying the whole thing. We contacted the doctor, who said I should get back on the antidepressants, but it was more a case of: how would I get through the start of term? And how would I manage the stress week after week?

'I didn't make the first week of term. I wasn't well enough. And when I did go back, I shared the workload. Peter had to go away on business at that time, which didn't help. His mum came and stayed while he was away. And I don't think the children noticed what was happening. We'd have told them I was finding things difficult and would have asked them for extra help around the house. But their lives continued as normal. Fiona is always busy going here, there and everywhere. And there were always meals on the table. Nothing at home was really so different.

'During that time I tried to relax. I tried to mind myself and not take on too much. It was difficult, but in the weeks while I waited for the medication to kick in, I had to be kind and nice to myself. That incident, though, made me realise that I had to get help for my anxiety.

'I started to see a women who advertised herself as a counsellor. It turned out she gave holistic therapies. She gave Reiki and taught courses. She practised a whole load of stuff. I went to her a couple of times, but I didn't feel we were connecting. Maybe I came across as someone who was managing a lot better than I was portraying to her.

'One day I was waiting outside her house, and I heard an energy psychologist, Sarah Bird, being interviewed by Gerry Ryan on his RTÉ morning show. What she was saying really registered with me. I went home that day and rang Sarah. And from the minute she spoke to me I sensed there was a connection there. I didn't feel she was too professional or official. There is, I feel, a fine balance between being professional, but at the same time being able to show some empathy. I wanted someone who was going to give me guidance and tell me that I would be fine. I sensed she was that person.

'Peter drove me to see her in Dublin. Sarah is brilliant! She gives you a bit of her life, too, so you don't feel as if it is me who has all the difficulties. We'll talk about whatever the issue is, and she starts to work on it straight away. She gives me tools, practical

❝ Going to Sarah feels like going to a counsellor, but you get more benefit. You feel she is actually doing something, rather than just talking about it ❞

things I can do on a daily basis. It's given me back some control. She uses a method called Emotional Freedom Therapy – or EFT. The theory behind EFT is that when you've had a negative experience, the body's bio-energy system gets disrupted. In order to remove the negative response, you tap into the bio-energy system using special positive statements. This releases the problem and balances your flow of energy. We'd practise the methods together, and she'd give me homework for the week.

'That first time she just listened and I cried. Peter sat in with me for the first four or five visits. I wanted to share with him what she had to say because he needed support too. I wasn't saying anything to Sarah that he would not have heard before, but I didn't want it seen as something I had in life that was completely separate to him.

'Soon I got to the stage where I felt Peter didn't have to come in with my any more. I felt I could manage it on my own. Sarah felt the same, even though we hadn't spoken about it. I still told Peter what we'd been talking about, but my need to share with him just wasn't as intense. At first I'd go to Sarah every week. I went each week for about two months. Now I go every five or six weeks. Sarah has made a huge difference to me. You'd not recognise the person I was when I went to her that first day.

'Life now is good. I still work, but I'm no longer in such a stressful job. I work with children with special needs for six days a week. It can be demanding, but I gain a huge amount from the children too. Ultimately, it's rewarding. Peter and I run an internet business; it's a sales website, and it's beginning to grow. Eventually I plan to run that full-time. These days I manage well on a day-today basis. I've learned to let things go. I used to feel frantic if the house wasn't perfect; now I can leave the kitchen floor for a while. I drive comfortably around the area, though I still find going to shopping centres a challenge. I tend to do my shopping on the spur of the moment. If it's not planned, I don't have time to think about it. Because the more time I have to think, the more likely it is to be problematic. Peter often spends a night away at weekends; he's keen on rallying, and I'm fine now at home when he's not there. We went to France again this year and it was a wonderful holiday. I was full of confidence and enjoyed every minute.

'I hope to get better still. I want to have the freedom to go wherever I want, without having to agonise about it. I've spent the past fifteen years building up to that. My ultimate goal is to drive and see Sarah without the need for Peter to come with me.

'My anxiety has been tough on Peter. He's had to be self-sacrificing, but you get to a stage where it becomes a way of life. If I say I want to go to such and such a place, he knows he'll have to be there to drive. We work around it. He's now telling me that I have to extend my boundaries, and I appreciate that. But in ways Peter has gained. I'm at home an awful lot more because of my anxiety and that means he is free to pursue his hobbies. If I get to a point where I say, "I'm away this weekend," he'll have to work around that.

'There's definitely a stigma around anxiety disorder. And I don't know if that will ever go away. There's a huge fear in Ireland about mental illness. It's like, "Oh God! Suppose that happened to me?" We run away from it. If people just thought about it for a while, if they maybe tried to embrace it, to understand and realise it happens for a reason, maybe the fear will go away. I know my anxiety is there as a sign that I need to get more harmony in my life.

'It's difficult to explain to people what panic feels like. Unless they've experienced it, they can't possibly imagine it. I find it's easier

❮ I'm careful whom I talk to about my anxiety. I've spent my time hiding it. Even now, there are only so many people I'll tell. People don't understand ❯

to talk to someone who thinks deeply about life. I've a good friend who lives abroad, someone I used to work with, and it's easy to talk to her.

'I've spent years trying to find a cure for my anxiety. I've been to see so many different people, and I've gained something from each one of them. Yet none of them can make it all right for me. I need support, but how I cope is very much down to me and my resources. It's a relief to accept that. It's scary in one way, but it's ultimately empowering.

'Coping is about realising how to run my life. I'm interested in politics; I like to know what's happening, but when it's all bad news,

❮ I've realised that there is no magic cure. I accept that the person who is going to cure me is me ❯

listening to the radio doesn't do me any good. Whatever will happen, will happen. There's absolutely nothing I can do about it. Getting myself wound up and depressed about the recession isn't going to change anything. So I try to keep my thoughts positive. I do all I can to keep my life harmonious.

'The other night I thought about watching Pat Kenny on *The Frontline*. Then I thought, no, it will be better for me if I go to bed now. I'll read inspirational cards or a book by Anthony de Mello. It's taken me a long time to realise I have control over my life, that I can decide to put my needs first.'

The things that helped

Attending an energy psychologist

- Of all the things I've tried over the years, this has been the most beneficial. I find the method Sarah Bird uses, Emotional Freedom Therapy, just brilliant.

Taking antidepressant medication

- The Effexor helps me to cope. I was determined to eventually come off the tablets, but I now accept that I need them. It no longer bothers me that I take them.

Owning a dog

- Our dog is the life and soul of our house. She's extremely placid and she's relaxing to be around. When I come in stressed from work, I'll go and sit with her for a few minutes and just stroke her. It's so calming. She has to be walked every day, and that's good for me too. She's been a wonderful addition to our family. We all love her and she loves us back unconditionally.

Aromatherapy

- I did a course in aromatherapy about fourteen years ago. I still use the oils. I find them hugely beneficial.

Reading self-help books

- I read them a lot, but if a book is no good, I'll stop reading halfway through. I like books by Eckhart Tolle, and I'll read anything by Louise Hay. I pick up some books time and again. I'll use them when things aren't going too well for me. They're great at grounding me and reminding me of important ways to cope.

Inspirational cards

- I keep my cards beside my bed. They give me positive statements to empower me before I go to sleep.

Switching off the radio

- I've stopped listening to the news when I wake up. I listen to Lyric FM instead. Classical music makes for a calm start to the day.

The things that didn't help

Acupuncture

- I tried acupuncture last summer when I came off my medication. I thought it might help me through, but it didn't seem to make any difference. I found the practitioner a bit intrusive. He talked a lot and I wanted to relax in silence.

Writing things down

- That has never done anything for me. I tried to do that, but seeing my thoughts in black and white makes them real. I want to leave my fear behind. There's no benefit, I find, in delving into it.

Margaret's Advice

1. Eat healthily. Get advice about your diet and about exercise.

2. Work at accepting yourself for the person you are.

3. Be as gentle with yourself as you would be with a new baby.

4. Try to surround yourself with people who have a positive attitude.

FOR MORE INFORMATION:
Sarah Bird, Supporting Change and Growth –
www.sarahbird.ie

CHAPTER FOURTEEN
Ned

Ned,* aged fifty, is a taxi-driver from County Wexford. Life today is good. Ned is happy. But at forty, after years of battling with anxiety, he experienced a severe psychotic episode and was sectioned into a psychiatric hospital.

*name has been changed

Ned adores his job as a taxi-driver. He loves chatting to people, loves being able to touch on so many different lives. People, he finds, open up to him. Often he hears tales of distress and depression, and although he's not prone to sharing his own story, he will let his customers know that he understands their pain. 'Sometimes I hint that I've suffered too. At the end of the journey I might say, "Don't give up. You will get through."'

Ned was born in England. His parents had moved there so that Ned's father could get work. But when Ned was five, his mother returned to Ireland, taking her three children with her. 'It was the typical emigrant thing,' says Ned. 'My father worked away all the time. He worked all over the place; we would see him only for holidays. My mother was a housewife and remained one for her entire life. When we came back to Ireland, we lived with my grandmother in Inch, near Gorey. Later we moved to a house in Gorey.

'Then my father developed cancer. He came home to the new house, but he was very sick with lung cancer. He died when I was fourteen. I never really had an opportunity to get to know him. The sickness had taken him over. We all went to the funeral. We were included in everything, but we never had the chance to mourn. There was no counselling for bereavement back then. We grieved in our own way, but I never actually dealt with my father's death.

'I became a wild child. I drank and I started taking drugs. I took cannabis, acid, the whole lot. I got into fighting too. My mother had no control over me. I was a pretty obnoxious bollocks actually. I was thrown out of school at fifteen. The main thing, though, was the drink. Once I started, I couldn't get enough of it. I joined a rock band with three friends. I loved that, but I was drinking way too much. One night when I was twenty-one, I walked into the local bar and I heard one of the lads say, "Oh no! Here comes Ned and he's pissed." That shocked me. It calmed me down for a while.

'Throughout that time I always worked. I was a marine electrician for a while. I hated that, and I became a sales rep. I stopped taking drugs in my early twenties, but I was still drinking copious amounts. I met my future wife when I was twenty-two and she was seventeen. We progressed from going out, to engagement, to marriage when I was twenty-five without really thinking about it. It was what you did.

'The marriage was never going to work. It was a mismatch between two very different people, but we had three beautiful daughters before we realised that. I

> ❛ It was St Patrick's Day 1993. The kids went to bed, and I was still there, but when they woke up I had disappeared ❜

wanted to be a family man and a good father. I wanted to stay in the marriage. I was determined to make it work, but we were totally incompatible. So it came to an end. It was nobody's fault, but that failure had a terrible traumatic effect on me.

'Two months later, the company I was working for folded. It was a double whammy. I was in bits. I was living in this poxy flat with £33 to live on. I used to sit in the flat freezing, saving the gas for when the girls came up at the weekends. It was fucking horrendous. I was back drinking too much again. My mother noticed. She said, "Please, son, don't turn to drink. It'll only make things worse." For some reason, her words sank in.

'I became good friends with a woman who had worked with me at the company that went bust. Shortly after that, her marriage broke up and we got together. All that, though, took a year, a year full of confusion. She was wondering should she give her marriage a chance. I was in such a bad way, and I hadn't got the wherewithal to get up and find a job. I was stuck in the situation. I hadn't the energy because of all the stuff going on – all the business with the family courts and the fights about the children. I started to get major panic attacks. I thought my heart would explode. Either that or I was going mad. I went to my doctor and he gave me tranquillisers.

> ❛ The tranquillisers calmed me down a bit, but it was like being caught in a sponge. The panic was still with me, but it was going on underneath the surface ❜

'My partner, Kate, and I decided to have a new start. So we went to London in 1994. We just set off with two cases, a carrier bag and no money. Kate had been to London before, so she knew her way around. We found some work. I got into sales. I started working my way up and was promoted and promoted. Before long I was dealing with corporate accounts, and it got very pressurised. That's when the stress started to reappear. It was terrible. I had panic attacks again and I couldn't concentrate. It became worse and worse. I ended up walking out of my job. I started with another company. I fluffed my way though the interview, but I didn't last long there. The panic came back. It was so bad that I went to a doctor who put me on the antidepressant Lustral. It made life bearable, but I was numb. That's the problem with medication.

'My kids had been over for the summer holidays. They'd been finding life in Ireland tough without me, so I made up my mind to go home. We returned in 1999, five years after we'd left. Kate, meanwhile, had become depressed. She was given medication but no other help. We were both in a mess when we got home.

'We lived in Ballycanew, County Wexford, to be out of town, but close enough to see my kids. I applied for a load of different jobs, and I started as a shift operator in Bray. We had to clock time and I couldn't stand it. Then I got a job in Gorey in a plastics company, working eight-hour shifts, including nights. That was tough, physical work, and I put out my back. That meant that I lost my job. I was angry about that, and I was stressed out of my head. The stress had been building for months and months. I was getting hyper, but I didn't really notice. I wasn't taking any medication at this stage. Kate was still deeply depressed. We were finding it hard to live with one another.

'My memory of this time is hazy, but life was pretty grim. I do remember that one night I called to our landlord's house and he gave me some whiskey. I hadn't drunk spirits in years, and I suspect it triggered something in me. Thinking back, I was pretty mad at that stage. I hadn't slept for nights and nights on end, and Kate just didn't know what to do with me. I walked into town and went on the piss for a few days. I ran amok. I turned a pub upside down and got everyone at loggerheads. Then I went to the garda station and said, "I am going to come back and kill you all." There were five gardaí there, and all they said was, "Get out, you mad bastard." I was standing in the street, screaming at the top of my voice, but they let me walk away.

'Next I walked to my GP's surgery. It wasn't far from the garda station. My GP was away; there was a stand-in there. I remember begging her for help and she said, "There is nothing I can do for you." At some stage, after that, I went back to Ballycanew. I was convinced that the television was talking to me and I wrote messages on walls all over the house. During those days, Kate had been in touch with our own GP. He wanted to admit me to a psychiatric hospital, but I refused to go. Kate was distraught and

❝ I remember holding the door handle and saying to the doctor, "One last time: I am begging you for help." And she said, "Have you tried the Samaritans?" ❞

she called my sister who, in turn, informed my mother. But my mother didn't know what to do; neither did my sister. Then my brother arrived on the scene and, between them, they decided their only option was to call the gardaí. I was saying that life didn't make sense and that I didn't make sense. I was totally out of my head.

'Two garda cars arrived. I invited the gardaí in, but when I realised what they were there for, I said I would cut their heads off. They handcuffed me, shoved me into the back of a squad car and the next thing I remember I was being driven through the gates of St Senan's Psychiatric Hospital in Enniscorthy. My poor mother had had to section me. That was a truly terrible thing. I was saying, "There is nothing wrong with me."'

❝ When you take drugs or alcohol, you're trying to make life positive all the time. At some point all that has to stop, because you have to experience the other side of life. All the time you drink or take drugs, you are not doing the growing up you should be doing ❞

Ned was forty at the time. Looking back, he believes that, until that time, he had never grown up. 'At thirty-five with a separation behind me, I realised I knew nothing at twenty-five,' he says. 'And when I was forty-five, I realised I'd known nothing at thirty-five. I was a heavy drinker throughout my thirties and forties. I was on the edge of being a true drug addict and a true alcoholic. I was on the edge of violence, but I never quite fell in.

'The day they handcuffed me was the day everything jumped up at me and slapped me across the face. That day will be with me until the end of my life, and I now thank God for it. Because I am now a completely different person. I could have gone on to be ninety years of age and not have been any wiser than I was at that time. I was so selfish. Life back then was all about me.

'I remember when we were going through the holding area in the hospital, everyone ignored me. It was as if I wasn't there. They brought me into this other place, and obviously I was quite agitated. They gave me a sedative. I didn't want it, but they jumped on me and gave it to me anyway. And I had a really bad reaction to it. My muscles went into spasm. My jaw clenched tight, like a rabid dog. My head locked down into my shoulders. I was curled up and my fists were clenched. My toes were curled under my feet. All my muscles seemed locked. I was scared shitless. I thought my heart would go into spasm. The only people in the room with me were my mother and my brother. This nurse came in and said, "Oh, he's having a reaction." Then he shut the door again and I thought, Oh Jesus! I was convinced I was going to die. Luckily he came back and gave me an injection to counteract the effect. I responded very fast.

'I was in St Senan's for a head-wrecking, soul-destroying month. To have your freedom taken away from you is unbearable. All the doors were locked. You couldn't smell the air. You had your medication in the morning and at night, and you interacted with the nurses. I basically shuffled through the month. The head doctor was a bitch of the highest order. She came round on Tuesday and Friday mornings. There was no interaction. And there was absolutely no counselling. You went in to see her and she filled in a questionnaire. You just tried to get the answers right. She'd check some ratchet on your arm; if there's not a fluid movement, it means you are not right. You'd be concentrating on: will I get out today? When you didn't get out, it was back to shuffling up and down the ward.

'My daughters were allowed to see me in hospital. It broke my heart for them to see me there. They were still young. They had, of course, noticed that something was wrong with Daddy and the way he was behaving, but they thought I was in an ordinary hospital.

> **❝ When you are depressed or have mental health problems, your whole way of viewing the world is bent out of shape. You can't see the world straight. And the terrible thing is that you can't make anyone else understand what it is that you feel ❞**

We told them I had hurt my back. Ob- viously, they know the truth now.

'Nobody ever told me what was wrong with me or if I would get better. They just leave you there. It was nonsense. And I had my forty-first birthday in hospital. In my final week they put me into a pre-release ward, and that was better. I actually had something to do, things like going to get the milk for breakfast-time. There wasn't any occupational therapy, and I mean nothing. There was an occupational therapy room, but the only things in it were half-completed jigsaws and wool. It was like a playschool basically.

'While I'd been in hospital, our landlord had chucked us out of the house in Ballycanew. We moved to Avoca and lived a good bit out of the village. It was too isolated out there, but maybe that was what I needed. For five weeks, when I'd been on that high, I was going to change the world. I believe that craziness was the nearest I have been to genius. Something happened. It was like a short circuit of everything that was inside me, and it changed me completely. I thought differently coming out of that.

'After I left the hospital, I was hit by horrendous depression. Nothing went on in my life. I just sat in the chair with my head bowed. I was in a terrible, terrible way, tearing myself apart inside. There was no point to my life. One thing though: I never, ever entertained the idea of suicide. I thought, I have three children. They need me, and they need me to provide for them. I wouldn't be able to do that if I remained as I was. I had to get better for them. The depression was really bad for about three months.

'Then a friend asked me to help him build a house. I think he asked me half to help me and half because he needed my help.

There were just the two of us there, and all the tradesmen, like plumbers and bricklayers, would come and go. That got me back into a bit of banter and made me feel human again. When we had finished the house, another friend wanted a paint job done. After that, I became a sheep farmer.

'I was on a very low dose of antidepressants. The doctors were afraid to give me more, in case it sent me back on to a high again. They didn't ever tell me what was wrong with me. But because I had changed districts, they sent me to an aftercare clinic in Rathdrum. I had a 3.30 p.m. appointment with the consultant psychiatrist on the last Wednesday of every month. You'd sit in the waiting room with the other twenty people who had a 3.30 p.m. appointment, and you'd see this guy for ten or fifteen minutes. He'd go down a checklist: "Do you sleep? How is your appetite?", and "Are you contemplating suicide?" I wanted to explore my thoughts, and I had to endure that regime for eighteen months because I didn't want to be thrown out of the medical system. I needed to play the game, but finally I could play it no more. I said to the consultant, "This isn't going to work. You are always going to be the doctor, and I am always going to be the patient. And while that's the case, there is no relationship, no trust. I don't want to be here."

'After I came out of hospital, I decided to explore why I'd become depressed and psychotic. What had made me into the person I was? I examined my family and our relationships and thought about my teens. We were a close family, but we didn't talk or confide in each other. We loved each other, but we didn't hug. I hadn't really talked to anyone about my father. We'd all found that difficult. And times were tough after he'd died. My mother was left with a new house, a mortgage and no income. She'd lost the man she loved at forty-three and had three children still in school. She turned two bedrooms into a flat to rent out, and my sister left school early so that she could contribute. We had no choice.

'I now think I'm very lucky, because I have an image of what my father was like. That is something for me to aspire to, rather than perhaps getting to know him and finding out how many faults he had. I have a knowledge of how he was kind, soft and a highly intelligent man. I am very much at peace with that now. And I did, once, learn a little more. I remember walking into a local pub and someone said he remembered my father. He said, "Jeez, he was some boy." He told me all this stuff about him and that made him seem more real.

'In the meantime I'd started a new job. I'd been offered some painting work for a few days, but it ended up being a job for a few years. I was happy but there was something missing. I thought about all the jobs I'd had – how I'd gone from sales to the plastics factory, to building, to sheep farming and back to building again. It didn't seem like much of a career. I realised that the problem was that I'd left school early and had never passed my Leaving Certificate. Whenever I went for an interview, I was always asked had I got it. That lack of qualification was following me from job to job. I went around for twenty-something years thinking, I'm stupid. I can't learn, I'm lacking intelligence.

'It was a huge risk when I decided to go back to school. This was two years after my breakdown and I was still feeling fragile. It took a massive amount of courage to sign up, because I had a horrendous fear of education, but it worked. To my surprise I absolutely loved it. I couldn't get enough of English, History and Biology, and I was good at it too. I flew my Leaving Certificate. During the course, which ran from 2002 until 2004, we were offered a counselling service to deal with the stress of exams. It was group therapy and was in Gorey. I used it as work for myself, for personal building, and I found it brilliant. After my Leaving

Certificate, I was encouraged to go to college. I decided to do a foundation course in counselling skills. I studied it through NUI Maynooth, at the satellite college St Thomas's in Bray. I felt I would make a good counsellor. I still feel that. Other people need the help that I didn't get. I believe I can help because I have first-hand knowledge of mental illness. I have a good understanding of what goes on inside people. I intend to become a counsellor, but I'm not ready just yet.

'The lecturer at St Thomas's recommended that we go to counselling. He felt it would be beneficial to us and a good opportunity to explore our own needs. One of the guys on the course had been seeing a counsellor called Caroline McGuigan in Arklow. I was now back living near Gorey, so he gave me her number. I've been seeing her ever since. It's been good. There are certain aspects of yourself that you will never otherwise discuss with another human being. Even when you are close to your partner, there are pieces you keep to yourself. I chat to Caroline quite a bit, and she will encourage me to explore my past. She can hand on things she has experienced or suggest that I read a certain book. She points me in the right direction, but in the end any healing comes from me.

'The counselling has definitely helped me. I've gained a lot of insight into why I was the way I was. I've come to terms with everything that has happened to me, and I've let go of my anger with people who were not there for me. I'm much closer to my family now. I see my mother every day. I help her with jobs around the house, and we drink copious amounts of tea. My relationships with all my family have become much closer since I became unwell. We're always there for each other.

'Two years ago I became a facilitator for the charity AWARE. And I've finally started a group in Gorey. That's brilliant because before that there were no groups between Bray and Enniscorthy. I went to a group once. It wasn't for me. I was in a low place and I think you need to feel a little stronger before these groups work for you. But it provides support for people who have really nothing else. And that once-a-week contact with people who are in a similar position can be a lifeline. They can share their experiences and explain how they got through the week. It brings someone a bit of peace. They get a glimpse of hope and of wellness, and they can then build on that.

'I now love my life. It's very simple. I have enough food, I have a house and I have good health. I've been with my partner now for sixteen years; we've helped each other through so much and we're still very happy together. I love her very much. I love my daughters too and their children. It's been wonderful to watch them grow. I'm learning to enjoy the now and not worry about the future or the past. I am happy. I still go out on the lash now and again. I get together with the lads, play pool, drink too much and wake up dying. I share an occasional bottle of wine with Kate too.

'I love my job most of the time. Being a taxi-driver is the greatest job in the world. I come into contact with all the diversity of life. I feel privileged to hear their stories, from the joy of a newborn baby to the death of someone through suicide. Some people don't want to talk. Others do and that's good because a taxi is like a confession box. I can make a way open for them to talk and be heard without being judged.

'And that is important. Because most people you approach when you are depressed don't want to know. They are afraid of mental health. They don't know what to say or how to deal with it. I've witnessed this with people I know, even casual people. Once you start to say how you feel, the shutters come down. You really are alone with depression. Only someone who has been through something similar can give you hope.'

The things that helped

Taking control of my own life

- I began to get well the day I said goodbye to the mental health services and took control of my own health.

Being involved with the peer support group AWARE

- Being able to support other people helps me enormously.

Counselling

- I was lucky to get counselling as part of my course. It can be expensive and is, I suspect, like a pair of shoes. You might have to try a few counsellors until you find one who suits you.

Going back to education

- Getting my Leaving Certificate and going to college were hugely important for me. It helped my self-esteem.

Music

- I love music. I bought a guitar a few months back. I hope I will become proficient at it. I'm often invited back to places when I'm driving my taxi. There was a sing-song in a pub one night, and I can actually sing. Someone said it was a waste that I don't use my voice and that night I decided I would start to.

Keeping active and seeing my friends

- I always try to keep busy. I've started playing chess every week. I'm really enjoying that.

Exercise
- We have two Jack Russell terriers. I walk them regularly. I go out to a beach and watch the seals. Being by the sea has always helped me.

The things that didn't help

The mental health service
- I had to learn to deal with my own problems.

Being unemployed
- That was one of the things that pushed me over the edge.

Drink
- For a long time I couldn't have a drink. Spirits and red wine, in particular, made me feel terrible for a few days. Now I can enjoy a drink without suffering ill-effects.

FOR MORE INFORMATION:

Along with her regular counselling work, Caroline McGuigan provides supports and services aimed at preventing suicide in Ireland. Having once attempted suicide herself, Caroline is Chief Executive Officer of Suicide or Survive. She runs courses in suicide prevention.

For more details, see www.suicideorsurvive.ie

APPENDIX

FURTHER READING

Bates, Tony, *Depression: The Common Sense Approach*, Gill & Macmillan, 1999

Cameron, Julia, *The Artist's Way: A Course in Discovering and Recovering Your Creative Self*, Pan Books, 1994

Corry, Michael and Áine Tubridy, *Depression: An Emotion, Not a Disease*, Mercier, 2005

de Mello, Anthony, *Awareness*, Zondervan, 1990

Dyer, Dr Wayne, *Pulling Your Own Strings*, Harper Torch, 1994

Lynch, Dr Terry, *Beyond Prozac: Healing Mental Suffering Without Drugs*, Second edition, Marino, 2005

Miller, Alice, *The Drama of Being a Child*, Virago, Revised edition, 1995

O'Callaghan, Gareth, *A Day Called Hope: A Personal Journey Beyond Depression*, New Island, 2004

Tubridy, Áine, *When Panic Attacks*, Gill & Macmillan, Second edition, 2008

SUPPORT GROUPS

AWARE www.aware.ie

A national voluntary organisation providing support for those coping with depression. Services include support groups nationwide and a LoCall Helpline open 365 days a year (both services are available to individuals with depression and also family members and friends). **Beat the Blues** is a secondary schools awareness programme, depression awareness and information talks and seminars and a free information service. For more information, call 01 661 7211, or email info@aware.ie.

GROW www.grow.ie

A mental health organisation which helps people who have suffered or are suffering from mental health problems. Members are helped to recover from all forms of mental breakdown or indeed to prevent such breakdowns from happening. GROW, founded in Australia in 1957 by former mental sufferers, has a national network of over 130 groups in Ireland. Its principal strength is the support members give each other from their own experience in mattersto do with mental health. GROW is grant-aided by the HSE and by the Department of Health and Children.

RECOVERY INTERNATIONAL www.recovery-inc-ireland.ie
A self-help group founded in Chicago, Illinois, in 1937 by the late
Dr Abraham A. Low. It offers the Recovery method of will training
for improved mental health and for control of nervous symptoms.
For more information, telephone (01) 6260775, email:
info@recovery-inc-ireland.ie or recovirl@indigo.ie.

OTHER HELPFUL WEBSITES

www.samaritans.org (1850 60 90 90)
The Samaritans provide confidential, non-judgemental emotional
support, 24 hours a day for people who are experiencing feelings
of distress or despair, including those which could lead to suicide.

www.Pieta.ie (01 6010000)

www.suicideorsurvive.ie
Suicide or Survive –The Centre for Prevention of Self-harm and
Suicide. Provides courses in suicide prevention.

www.pnd.ie (021 4923162)
Post Natal Depression Ireland – provides support, help and
friendship to those suffering from post-natal depression

www.imba.ie.
The Irish Multiple Birth Association – offers a unique insight into
the issues facing expectant parents and families of multiples during
pregnancy, birth and the different stages of childhood.

SUPPORT FOR THE ELDERLY

Senior Helpline

The Senior Help Line
www.seniorhelpline.ie (1850 440 444).

Age and Opportunity

Age and opportunity – for details of classes for older people,
see www.olderinireland.ie.

SUPPORT FOR TEENAGERS

Headstrong

The National Centre for Youth Mental Health –
www.headstrong.ie.

The No Name Club

A national voluntary youth organisation that aims to
provide an alternative to the pub culture –
www.nonameclub.ie.

Teen-Line Ireland

A listening service for teens in distress – www.teenline.ie.

Other websites

www.letsomeoneknow.com
www.spunout.ie

ABOUT THE THERAPIES

Counselling

The National Counselling Institute of Ireland –
www.ncii.ie.

Cognitive Behavioural Therapy

Cognitive Behavioural Therapy (CBT) – www.cognitive.ie – is
based on the idea that how we think (cognition), how we act
(behaviour), how we feel (emotion) and what is happening in
our bodies (physiology) interact together. Specifically, our
thoughts strongly influence our feelings and our behaviour;
therefore unhelpful, negative and unrealistic thoughts can be a
major source of distress.

Reiki

The word Reiki – www.reiki.ie – comes from two Japanese
words, Rei and Ki. Rei may be interpreted as supernatural
knowledge or spiritual consciousness. This is the wisdom that
comes from God or the Higher Self. This wisdom knows the
cause of all problems and how to heal them. Ki is the life force,
the non-physical energy that animates all living things. Reiki
may be defined as spiritually guided life-force energy. A Reiki
healer acts as a channel between the wisdom and the patient.
The healer has no influence on the degree of healing but simply
facilitates the flow of energy to where it is best needed.

Mindfulness

Mindfulness–www.breathworks-mindfulness.org.uk,
www.mindfulness-ireland.org – is the energy of being aware and
awake to the present moment. It is the continuous practice of
touching life deeply in every moment of daily life. To be mindful
is to be truly alive and present with those around you and with
what you are doing. We bring our body and mind into harmony
while we wash the dishes, drive the car or take our morning cup
of tea.

Aromatherapy

Aromatherapy – www.wellbeing.ie – uses pure essential oils to promote health and counteract diseases. This massage treatment works on the physical body through specially designed movements to improve circulation and encourage lymph drainage, helping to clear waste and toxins. It is effective for anxiety and depression.

Emotional Freedom Technique

Emotional Freedom Technique (EFT) – www.eftireland.net – involves holding a disturbing memory or emotion in mind and simultaneously using the fingers to tap on a series of twelve acupoints on the body. The theory behind EFT is that when a negative experience occurs, negative emotions are felt and the body's bio-energy system gets disrupted, which leads to inappropriate programming inside the body. In order to remove the negative responses, you tap into the bio-energy system using specific cognitive statements relating to the issue. This releases the problem and brings the body's energy field into balance, allowing your natural positive energy to flow.